Life in an Italian prisoner-of-war camp was primitive and demoralising – but captured Allied servicemen soon established a comradely existence, concentrating on improving their living conditions, on sports, camp entertainment . . . and escape. It was the duty of every prisoner to try to escape and rejoin his regiment – but the penalty for failure was high, for both the escaper and the rest of the camp. And even if successful, a bid for freedom was fraught with danger . . . from enemy guns, and from betrayal . . .

Jack Bishop

In Pursuit of
Freedom

CORGI BOOKS
A DIVISION OF TRANSWORLD PUBLISHERS LTD

IN PURSUIT OF FREEDOM
A CORGI BOOK 0 552 10573 2

Originally published in Great Britain by
Leo Cooper Ltd.

PRINTING HISTORY
Leo Cooper edition published 1977
Corgi edition published 1977

This book is set in Intertype Baskerville

Corgi Books are published by
Transworld Publishers Ltd,
Century House, 61–63 Uxbridge Road,
Ealing, London W5 5SA
Made and printed in Great Britain by
Cox & Wyman Ltd., London, Reading and Fakenham

CONTENTS

In Pursuit of Freedom

I. SUBMARINE SERVICE

It was July, 1937, and I was in Hong Kong serving as a Seaman Gunner in HMS Submarine *Perseus* of the 4th Submarine Flotilla, China Fleet. Submarines destined to serve in that part of the world were specially built to withstand the conditions out there, where they would remain for the whole of their useful working life. Crews would normally serve for periods of two and a half years, travelling to and from Hong Kong in troopships.

Two such submarines, *Oswald* and *Osiris*, having apparently reached the end of their working lives, were leaving for England and as was customary, the crews of other submarines had gathered on the quay wall to wish them *bon voyage*.

It was a sad occasion for me, because I had served in *Osiris* and had become fond of her. When she cast off her moorings and there was a call for three cheers, it was like cheering at an old friend's funeral. Little did I realize how wrong I was in thinking that they were to be scrapped. It was destined that I should meet them again before long and indeed serve in one of them.

I continued in the *Perseus* until November, 1938, when, having completed my term of service, I was relieved from duty and sailed for Southampton in the troopship *Lancashire*. When my leave expired I reported to the Submarine Base at Fort Blockhouse in Gosport, from whence I was sent to join HM Submarine *Triumph* which was being built at the shipyard of Vickers Armstrong at Barrow-in-Furness.

Some three months later when she was completed and trials had proved satisfactory, we sailed for Fort Blockhouse.

9

There, to my surprise, were the *Oswald* and *Osiris*. Since their arrival from Hong Kong they had lain in Portsmouth Dockyard and had recently been brought to Fort Blockhouse to be re-commissioned. It was June, 1939, and the possibility of war with Germany had become very real. This was the reason for the reprieve of these craft.

I had been sent to the *Triumph* because, at twenty-nine I was one of the more experienced ratings needed to take her through her trials. Having completed my task, I was sent back to Fort Blockhouse to await another drafting. I was quite happy with that arrangement because it was rumoured that the *Triumph* was being sent on foreign service and I felt that I deserved a spell at home. I did not feel quite so happy, two days later, when I was ordered to join the *Oswald*. She was long overdue for the shipbreakers and so hardly a fair exchange for the *Triumph*. Ironically, the *Triumph* it was that remained on home service while the *Oswald* sailed for foreign seas.

The *Oswald* was one of six 'O' Class submarines. They were vessels of 1,200 tons, 283 feet in length, and with a beam of 28 feet. They had eight torpedo tubes – six in the bow, and two in the stern. Seven spare torpedoes could also be carried. One 4-inch gun and two Lewis guns completed the armament. Five officers and fifty men comprised the crew.

Having lain idle in Portsmouth Dockyard for nearly two years, the *Oswald* was in a sorry state and the crew had to work hard to get her clean and seaworthy. She was taken to sea for trials and on submerging for the first time she did not stop until she hit the sea bed. Fortunately, it was in only 60 feet of water and she surfaced without difficulty. I did not know what had gone wrong and I am sure that no one else did. It was the first of many similar, rather unnerving experiences.

Orders were finally given for the submarine to join the Submarine Depot ship HMS *Forth* at Dundee. A Submarine Depot ship is equipped with elaborate workshops and machinery, and carries out any repairs required by the submarines attached to her. Crews live aboard her while in harbour, and she can also supply the submarines with fresh water, oil, fuel, food, stores and ammunition.

Shortly after joining the *Forth*, the *Oswald* was despatched to undertake a fourteen days' submerged patrol in the Skagerrak. There were two likely explanations for this – firstly to give the crew, who were all new to the submarine, the experience of being on patrol – and secondly, as war with Germany was now a matter of grave concern, to give the Captain the opportunity to observe the movements of any German craft in the area.

On completion of the patrol, the submarine returned to the *Forth* and normal routine was resumed until 1 am on Wednesday, 21 August, when the crew were roused from their sleep and told to report to the submarine where we were ordered to prepare for sea under war conditions.

In preparing the *Oswald* for war, the dummy 'blowing' heads on the torpedoes had to be replaced by warheads. Food and stores to last a month were embarked and fresh water tanks and oil fuel tanks were filled to capacity. Ammunition for the gun was also embarked. At 5 pm, when the Captain was satisfied that the submarine was ready for sea, he reported to the Senior Submarine Officer in the *Forth* who gave orders to proceed.

The Captain did not divulge our destination, but at 9 am on Friday, 24 August, the submarine arrived at Fort Blockhouse where he went ashore. Returning shortly afterwards he gave orders for the submarine to be ready for sea again at noon. On sailing, a southerly course was set and, at 4 pm on the following Tuesday, the submarine arrived at Gibraltar, remaining only long enough to top up fresh water and oil fuel tanks. On sailing at six, she headed into the Mediterranean, and it became known that she was bound for Malta.

Italy had formed an alliance with Germany and so it was necessary to sail with extreme caution. A good lookout had to be maintained and if any ships were sighted the submarine had to submerge. The island of Pantelleria, which lies off the coast of Tunisia, was an Italian air and sea-plane base and, to avoid being sighted by aircraft, the Captain decided to pass the island submerged – at a depth of 300 feet. The reason for such a depth was that in the clear water of the Mediterranean a submarine is visible from the air to a depth of 100 feet, while at 200 feet the outline can still be made out. That, I think, explains why so many of our submarines were sunk in the Mediterranean during the war.

Unfortunately things did not quite work out according to plan. The hull of a submarine – known as the pressure hull – is cigar-shaped and very little of it is visible above the surface of the water. What one sees is a casing which floods with water when the submarine submerges and drains when she surfaces, and is the stowage for mooring ropes and wires. The way in, and out, of the submarine is through round hatches measuring approximately 30 inches in diameter. In the *Oswald*, if one needed to embark anything that was too big to go through the hatches, it was possible to detach a steel plate measuring 6 feet by 4 feet from the top of the pressure hull.

On submerging, we reached a depth of 200 feet when there was a loud crack and a sudden inflow of water. The Captain ordered an immediate return to the surface where it was discovered that the removable steel plate had buckled, causing some of the securing bolts to snap. We could no longer sail submerged and a signal was sent to Malta requesting dry-dock facilities immediately on arrival. Fortunately no aircraft were flying from Pantelleria at the time. The *Oswald* had been designed to submerge to a far greater depth than 200 feet and I must confess that I was a little disturbed by this mishap. I remember thinking what would have happened had we been at war and the submarine was attacked by an enemy ship. She would have had to surface to avoid flooding, where she would have been a sitting target for enemy gun-fire.

Arriving at Malta early in the morning of Sunday, 3 September, the submarine was immediately dry-docked. The crew had just settled down in their mess to enjoy a well-earned cigarette and their rum ration when the First Lieutenant arrived and quietly announced that England had declared war on Germany.

I do not fear death but I must confess that, on receiving the First Lieutenant's announcement that we were at war, I felt a little uneasy. I considered the *Oswald* to be no more than a heap of scrap metal in which I had no confidence. If I had to die, which was a possibility, I wanted an opportunity to fight for my life.

The task of fitting a new plate to the pressure hull of the *Oswald* took two days and she was then moved from the dry-dock to the Submarine Base at Fort Manoel in Lazaretto Creek where the crew landed their personal belongings and took up residence. The *Osiris* had followed us to Malta and we were the only two warships there. I had known Malta in happier times while serving with the Mediterranean Fleet, but on this occasion, with the Fleet away, life was far from happy. A destroyer popped in occasionally and we would give her practice in searching for a submerged submarine, but this was just about the extent of our activity.

There was a break in the monotony a fortnight before Christmas when the *Oswald* was ordered to proceed to sea for a fortnight on Contraband Patrol. This entailed searching the sea for cargo ships carrying enemy war material. If any had been located they would have been escorted into Malta where ship and cargo would have been confiscated. Our search proved fruitless, however, and the *Oswald* returned to Malta in time for the crew to spend Christmas.

Shortly after Christmas the First Lieutenant of the *Oswald* was ordered home to England to take his Commanding Officer's course. He was successful and assumed command of a submarine, but, much to our sorrow, we heard that on her first patrol under his command she had been sunk without trace by enemy action.

13

Despite the many shortcomings of the *Oswald*, she possessed at least one priceless asset: a good Commanding Officer, Lieutenant-Commander Sladen. As I had joined the Submarine Service in 1935, I knew most of the Commanding Officers and potential Commanding Officers who distinguished themselves during the war and I admired and respected them all, but none more than Sladen. He was a born leader and a most efficient submarine officer. He absolutely radiated confidence and gave one the impression that, come what may, he would win through. It was therefore with a feeling of sadness that I learnt that he, too, was leaving the *Oswald* to return to England. On his arrival he was given command of HM Submarine *Trident* where he distinguished himself particularly on Arctic Patrols. He was subsequently appointed to select and train crews for the Midget Submarines that played such an important part in the war. His successor, as Commanding Officer of the *Oswald*, was Lieutenant-Commander Fraser.

On resuming the routine of proceeding to sea to play hide and seek with visiting destroyers, the *Oswald* introduced a little variety into the proceedings. She was very seldom in trim, by which, I mean that she was seldom on an even keel. Valves that should have operated to allow the passage of water in or out of the ballast tanks sometimes stuck and this caused the submarine to sink by her bow or stern. There were occasions when she would go through the water like a porpoise and I sometimes thought that she would loop the loop.

The principle of a submarine is that when it is required to submerge, tanks, known as Main Ballast tanks, are flooded with water, and when it is required to surface the water is blown out by compressed air. These tanks are external and are situated each side of the submarine and when she is on the surface the tops are just visible which gives her a bloated appearance. Not all of these tanks are ballast tanks, however, some are oil-fuel tanks, and others fresh water tanks. The *Oswald* had eight of these tanks on each side. In preparing a submarine to submerge it is necessary, first of all, to apply the trim. This is usually done in harbour and is to ensure that when the submarine submerges, she does so gracefully and in complete control. In applying the trim, allowances have to be made for any extra weight carried in excess of that allowed for in the design of the craft. Allowances have to be made for the amount of food, torpedoes, fresh water, ammunition, and also for any passengers carried. This is done by pumping water into or out of auxiliary tanks situated inside the submarine at the bottom. In the *Oswald* these tanks were 'A' and 'B' in the forward part and 'X' and 'Y' in the after part. In the midships section were 'O' Port and 'O' Starboard; these tanks were used to correct any list. The oil fuel tanks were fitted with a compensating system which allowed water to take the place of the oil fuel as it was used.

The external main ballast tanks were fitted with two valves – one in the top known as a Main Vent and the other in the bottom known as a Kingston Valve. The second stage in preparing the submarine to submerge is to open all Kingstons, which would allow the tanks to flood with water until air in them was compressed to its limit, when flooding would cease. The submarine, although losing some of her buoyancy, would remain on the surface and would then be said to be 'riding on her vents'. The final stage is to open the Main Vents which will allow the air in the tanks to escape and the tanks to flood with water completely. This action destroys positive buoyancy and reduces the submarine to a state of neutral buoyancy when she will then glide steadily downwards, assisted by the hydroplanes.

The hydroplanes are horizontal rudders situated forward and aft on each side of the submarine. They measure approximately 8 feet by 4 and their function is to assist the submarine to submerge and surface, and to assist in maintaining depth and trim while submerged. When a submarine is submerged and in perfect trim, it should be possible, in theory, to grasp one of her periscopes in one hand and lift her up and down. To bring the submarine to the surface the main vents are shut and the water in the tanks is blown out through the Kingstons by compressed air. This restores positive buoyancy and with the hydroplanes at 'hard to rise' she will then rise in a level position to the surface.

In the *Oswald* compressed air was stowed in steel bottles at a pressure of 3,000 pounds to the square inch. There were thirteen of these bottles and they were distributed in groups of twos and threes throughout the submarine. They were all connected to a steel pipe known as the HP (High Pressure) Air Line which ran the whole length of the submarine with branches leading from it into the Main Ballast Tanks. In blowing water out of the tanks, a pressure a little in excess of the sea pressure is all that is required. If the full pressure of 3,000 pounds to the square inch was used the tanks would burst.

Nothing happened to relieve the quietness of life at Malta until May when orders were given for the crew to transfer their personal belongings to the submarine and prepare for sea. This indicated a move away from Malta and the more optimistic of the crew thought that we were returning to England. It was not so, however; our destination proved to be Alexandria in Egypt.

Conflict eventually came to the Mediterranean in June when Italy declared war on England. Air raids became a nightly occurrence and submarines quietly departed to seek out and destroy their prey. The *Oswald* was dispatched on patrol a few days after the declaration of war. She departed at dusk on a northerly course, sailing on the surface throughout the night. At dawn the next day she submerged and proceeded on the same course throughout the day. As darkness fell she surfaced, and that henceforth was the routine – submerged by day and on the surface at night.

On the first day of the patrol it was noticed that the fresh water had a salty taste and on investigation, it was discovered that a bulkhead separating a fresh water tank from a salt water tank had collapsed, thereby rendering 2,000 gallons of fresh water unfit for human consumption. The *Oswald* was indeed running true to form! Fresh water rationing was introduced forthwith and, if I remember rightly, the ration was one pint per man per day. The contaminated water could be used for ablutions but, as soap will not lather in salt water, not much benefit was derived from having a wash.

The remainder of the voyage passed without incident and we eventually arrived at the entrance to the Dardanelles, where we were to attack any enemy craft we encountered. Patrol Routine was put into operation and this entailed patrolling an area one mile square – submerged by day and on the surface at night. Only one third of the crew were required to man the submarine and were therefore organized into three watches – Red, White and Blue. Two hour watches were operated which meant that the crew were on watch for two hours and off for four.

Conditions when submerged were very unpleasant. The air trapped in the submarine when she submerged was all that the crew had to breathe until she surfaced again. It could not be added to because it would build up a pressure which would be injurious to the crew, neither could it be purified. To conserve it many restrictions had to be imposed. Smoking was forbidden and those of the crew off watch were not allowed to move about as the extra effort required would entail heavier breathing. Cooking of food was also forbidden because of the smell that would pollute the air, and the undue heat that it would produce. When submerged the submarine was propelled by electric motors – the electricity being stored in batteries – and this also had to be used as sparingly as possible because the submarine would remain submerged for at least eighteen hours and there was always the possibility that she might come under attack and would have to remain submerged even longer. As a further measure to conserve electricity, all unnecessary lights were switched off which ruled out reading as a way of passing away the time. Members of the crew off watch had to either sit or lie still because if they moved about they would upset the balance of the submarine. The one cooked meal that was provided in each twenty-four hours was cooked on the surface at night. Cold food was provided when submerged and I well remember the menu – tinned bacon and tinned tomatoes, or tinned pilchards in tomato sauce. Even now I shudder when I think of it.

To relieve the monotony while on patrol we played card games, chess and draughts and on this particular patrol a beard growing competition was organized. The rules were simple – entrants had to pay an entrance fee of fifty cigarettes and not shave for the duration of the patrol. First prize was 75 per cent of the cigarettes and the remaining 25 per cent was for the booby prize. The judge of the competition was the Captain.

It was the practice to submerge the submarine at 4 am and bring her to the surface at 10 pm. She patrolled at periscope depth and careful observation was kept by the Officer of the Watch through the periscopes throughout the day. He would raise one periscope at frequent intervals and after taking a careful all-round sweep would lower it again. It was never allowed to remain up.

The most dangerous period for the submarine was immediately after submerging and again just prior to surfacing at night. It was at those times when the light was bad that she was most vulnerable to an attack from surface craft. To overcome that danger it was the practice to take her to ninety feet. During this period all white electric lamps would be replaced by blue ones in order to get the crew's eyes used to the semi-darkness. When the Captain was ready to surface he would order the submarine to be brought to periscope depth and would then take careful observation through the periscope. He could not see much but there was the possibility that he might catch a glimpse of a betraying light from any surface craft that happened to be there. On satisfying himself that all was well he would give the order to surface and, followed by the signalman, would mount the ladder leading into the conning tower. It was possible that during the day, due to leaks in the air system, a pressure had built up inside the submarine and great care had to be exercised in opening the conning tower hatch. This was done by the Captain and, to avoid the possibility of him being swept out of the submarine when the pressure was released, the signalman would grasp him around his legs to anchor him.

On reaching the bridge they would both take careful observation through their binoculars and if any surface craft had been sighted the signalman would make the challenge by Aldis Lamp. The challenge was a three letter signal and was made in Morse Code. It was known to all friendly ships and was changed every four hours. If no reply was made by the surface craft it would be assumed that she was hostile and she would be attacked. On satisfying himself that all was well the Captain would order Patrol Routine, which was the most welcome order given. It meant that the crew could carry on smoking and the rum ration be issued; it was also the signal for the cook to start cooking.

Much had to be done while the submarine was on the surface, the most important tasks being to charge the batteries and air bottles. One of the two diesel engines would be run in opposition to one of the electric motors, thereby generating electricity, while the other was used for propulsion. A compressor was also run to charge the air bottles before the next descent beneath the surface.

After a fortnight of patrolling, we were ordered to return to Alexandria. Orders had been given for the submarine to remain in harbour for one week when she was to be ready for sea again. During that period much work had to be done. Food, fresh water and oil-fuel had to be embarked and the craft had to be thoroughly overhauled. The submarine was ready for sea at the appointed time but orders to proceed were not forthcoming. No explanations were given for the delay, and it was not until the evening of 18 July that she finally received her sailing orders.

On clearing Alexandria harbour a westerly course was set and, as on previous occasions, the submarine proceeded on the surface throughout the night and submerged at dawn the next day. Once again the crew were kept in ignorance as to our destination.

The crew very quickly settled down once again to Patrol Routine. Nothing untoward happened on this voyage and on arriving at our destination, the Straits of Messina, an area one mile square was patrolled. The Straits of Messina are the narrow strip of water between the toe of Italy and Sicily, a very hot spot to be in.

It was at daybreak on 29 July, just after the submarine had submerged, that the Officer of the Watch sighted smoke on the horizon which indicated that a ship was approaching. He sent for the Captain who, after taking a look through the periscope, ordered the crew to Diving Stations. The *Oswald* went forth into battle for the first time.

The Captain said nothing for five minutes or so; there then followed a series of announcements that went something like this – 'I can see a mast', 'I can see another mast', 'I can see a funnel', 'Another mast', 'Another funnel', 'I can see a ship that looks like a cruiser', 'It is a cruiser', 'I can see another cruiser', and in rapid succession 'A destoyer', 'Another destroyer', 'A ship that looks like a troopship', 'Another troopshop', 'Another cruiser', 'Another destroyer'. There was then a short pause and then the final announcement which was 'Enemy force of four cruisers, four destroyers and two troopships in sight bearing Red 10'. I had been under the impression that the whole Italian fleet had been sighted. There was complete silence in the Control Room broken only by the sound of the Captain's voice and the gentle hiss of the telemotor system as the periscope was raised and lowered.

The Captain ordered an alteration in course and an increase in speed which indicated that he was going to attack. The target was to be the leading troopship which was steaming line ahead with the other troopship, with the cruisers and destroyers forming a protective screen around them. To get into an attacking position the submarine had to penetrate the protective screen and it was done with such ease, at a depth of 90 feet, that I wondered what the crews of the cruisers and destroyers were doing to allow it. They must have been keeping some sort of listening watch for submarines and how the *Oswald* escaped detection I just do not know.

A torpedo has to be fired some distance ahead of its moving target and the angle of firing – called the DA or Director Angle – is established by making calculations from information that can be obtained concerning the relative speeds and directions of the two vessels. The torpedo and target should then cross each other's path simultaneously.

I had taken part in many practice attacks in peacetime and I had found them rather boring. My main thoughts had been to get them over with as soon as possible so that the submarine could return to harbour and I could go ashore. But this attack was the real thing and was a very different kettle of fish. Many thoughts crossed my mind as we approached the enemy, the chief of which was that I might be going to my death. I am not a very religious type, but I remember reciting to myself what I remembered, of my then favourite Psalm, 'The Lord is my Shepherd I shall not want'. I also recall saying my farewells to my wife and children. It occurred to me for the first time what a cowardly method of warfare submarine warfare really was. Here was the *Oswald* creeping below the surface and being manoeuvred into position to deliver a death blow to perhaps 1,000 men. It seemed to me totally opposed to the English conception of fair play. However, I found some consolation in the fact that the *Oswald* was alone and was attacking such a formidable force.

The enemy was steering a zig-zag course in order to upset the calculations of potential attackers. The Captain had ordered all torpedo tubes to be brought to the ready and had indicated that he intended firing four of the six bow torpedoes. Just when it appeared that he was going to fire he released a sudden flow of oaths. He had missed his attack. The target had altered course on its zig-zag just as the torpedoes were to be fired. The submarine was then swung completely round in an endeavour to deliver an attack with the two stern torpedoes but this also failed and she was swung back again. While all this was going on the target was moving rapidly away and would soon be out of range. Rapid calculations were made and the torpedoes were fired more or less at random, almost at extreme range.

The normal procedure when firing torpedoes was for the submarine to be kept at periscope depth long enough for the Captain to observe the result of his attack and then, if there was a danger of a reciprocal attack, he would order a depth of 300 feet and, with the motors running at full speed, would take such evasive action as he thought necessary. On this occasion, however, things did not quite work out as they should have done because, when the torpedoes were fired, the *Oswald* – for no apparent reason and once again running true to form – dropped like a stone and was at 200 feet before she could be checked. To return to periscope depth would have then been a waste of valuable time so a depth of 300 was ordered and with the motors running at full speed, which gave the submarine a speed of eight knots, she proceeded to make herself scarce.

There then followed an almost unbearable pause in the proceedings – the time that the torpedoes would take to reach their objective – and it was some three minutes after their firing that the reports of two terrific explosions were heard and we then knew that two of the torpedoes had found their mark. It was then anticipated that the cruisers and destroyers would make a combined attempt to locate the submarine and destroy her by depth-charge attacks. I do not think that the crew of the *Oswald* had ever listened more intently for signs of approaching danger as they did on that occasion. There was complete silence with everyone hardly daring to breathe. I think that everyone – even the most un-Christian – felt nearer to God at that particular time than they can ever have before. The submarine continued to move away from the scene of the attack and when signs of approaching danger were not forthcoming there was first a feeling of relief among the crew and then of bewilderment. We could not understand why the expected depth charge attack did not materialize. Perhaps they were bound for North Africa, carrying troops to take part in the desert war, besides the troops being carried in the troopships there were others in the cruisers and destroyers. Perhaps the Senior Officer, having lost one ship by submarine attack and not knowing how many submarines there were, had considered it wiser to press on rather than hunt submarines and lay his force open to further losses.

When it was considered safe to do so, speed was reduced and the submarine continued to vacate the area in a more leisurely manner. A depth of 300 feet was maintained but some two hours after the attack and when he considered it safe to do so, the Captain decided to return to periscope depth. After taking a good look through the periscope he announced that there was nothing in sight and ordered the crew to fall out from Diving Stations and for Watch Diving Stations to be resumed. It was not known if the troopship had sunk and as the submarine returned to the patrol area a careful lookout was kept by the officer of the Watch, through the periscope, for any sign of her or of wreckage. Nothing was sighted and we did not know what had happened to her. However, we had engaged the enemy in action for the first time and had scored hits with two torpedoes. (We were told some time later that the troopship had been sunk).

On the afternoon of the following day an aircraft was sighted as it flew over the submarine, then lying at periscope depth. We had certainly been spotted. After the events of the previous day it was obvious that this aircraft had been sent to look for the submarine and, having located her, was now on its way back to report. Further action could now be expected.

No further sightings were made during the rest of that day, or on the following day, but shortly after eleven o'clock at night the alarm was again raised. It was a dark night with no moon or stars and we had been on the surface for an hour when the lookouts sighted the dark shape of a ship, showing no lights, passing on the port side on an opposing course. The Captain, who was in the wardroom helping to de-code signals, was sent for, but by the time he reached the bridge the craft had disappeared. It soon became clear, however, that the submarine had been sighted because this unknown ship was next observed steaming straight at our starboard side with the obvious intention of ramming us. Our Captain immediately ordered an alteration of course to port, and an increase in speed, in an attempt to bring the submarine on the same course as the approaching ship and so present as small a target as possible. He then shouted down the voice pipe to the Control Room 'Stand by to abandon ship' followed closely by the order 'Abandon ship'.

These orders were not immediately obeyed because the submarine was then struck a terrific blow on her starboard quarter which caused her to heel to port at an alarming angle. The crew were thrown off balance with all the loose fittings and gear falling on top of them. I had been having a sponge down in the wash-place when the alarm was raised and I had hurriedly donned shorts and sandals, which was all I wore when at sea. When the submarine was struck I was in the crew space and I was thrown up against the ship's side with the mess gear falling on top of me. Luckily I was not hurt. The attacking ship could then be heard as she scraped her way along the starboard side of the submarine and there then followed the sound of two terrific explosions, one aft and one forward, which was the report of two exploding depth charges. I was momentarily deafened and I thought that my eardrums had been damaged. The lighting failed and all machinery stopped. Blue flashes of light were shooting out all over the place as fuses were blown as if in a firework display.

Only those members of the crew in the immediate vicinity of the Control Room had heard the order to 'Abandon ship'. Everything had happened with such rapidity that there had not been time to pass orders and those of the crew in other parts of the submarine were in complete ignorance as to what was happening. Orders were normally passed by the telephone but this had been put out of action by the enemy's depth charges. I heard Lieutenant Pope, the Gunnery Officer, calling my name and when I answered he told me to open up the Gun Tower hatches and get out of the submarine as quickly as possible. He then went fore and aft telling everyone to get out, and as he did not know what damage had been done to the submarine, nor even if she would remain afloat, his conduct was praiseworthy indeed.

I mounted the ladder leading to the lower hatch of the Gun Tower and opened the lid without difficulty. With other members of the crew following me, I climbed through into the tower and up the second ladder leading to the upper hatch. I released the securing clips with ease but could not open the lid. There was a coaming around the hatch, and fixed to the lid where it rested on the coaming was a strip of rubber forming a water-tight joint. It seemed as though the pressure of water when the submarine was submerged had caused the rubber to stick. I was working under extreme difficulty because the ladder was straight and I had to hold on to it with one hand to support myself and work with the other. I managed to wedge myself so that I was able to use both my hands, and with a tremendous heave I managed to open it. I lost no time in scrambling out on to the Gun Platform where I was quickly joined by those of my shipmates who were behind me in the tower.

I had been so engrossed in my endeavour to open the lid that I had completely forgotten the predicament that we were now in. I had come that way out of the submarine on many occasions, when practising gun drill, but I was soon brought face to face with a new sort of reality when I saw the flash and heard the report of gun fire and saw tracer ammunition whizzing overhead. I quickly clambered over the gun shield and dropped down to the casing and then to the starboard external main ballast tanks on the blind side. I could smell oil fuel which indicated a leakage. Cloud that had previously obscured the moon began to break up and we had flashes of moonlight enabling us to catch fleeting glimpses of the enemy ship that had now started to circle the submarine at high speed, firing her guns as she did so. I could see that she was a small type of destroyer. There was no point in remaining on the external tanks so I climbed back on to the casing and joined others of my shipmates. Everyone was in a complete state of bewilderment; it all seemed a bad dream.

The only life-saving equipment provided in the submarine was the Davis Submerged Escape Apparatus, which, as the name suggests, was really for escape from a submerged submarine, but with the breathing bag inflated it could be used on the surface as a life jacket. Some of the crew had brought theirs with them but those of us who had not did not feel inclined to go back for them.

The Captain shouted to us from the bridge that at a given signal from him we were to take to the water on the port side. He told us that he would take a torch with him; when we saw the flash of his torch, or heard his shout, we were to swim towards him to ensure that when the destroyer stopped to pick us up no one would be left behind. In thinking that we would be picked up he was more optimistic than his crew.

The submarine was now in a sorry plight. Her main engines and main motors had been put out of action and she was a sitting duck for the guns of the enemy ship. It was quite an ordeal to stand on the casing and watch the shells whizzing overhead and we were all glad when the Captain gave the order to take to the water. I swam about a hundred yards and then turned around. I was just in time to see the submarine disappear below the surface of the water.

That, then, was the sad and inglorious end of the *Oswald*. She had been abandoned by her crew without firing one shell, or one torpedo, in her defence.

II. CAPTURE

THE water was warm and calm, but after a while we discovered that we were swimming in oil fuel that had leaked
from the damaged tanks of the *Oswald*. It was thick, like
treacle, and I had difficulty in keeping it out of my eyes and
mouth. I kept close to the Captain in the water and saw that
he was carrying the Engineer Officer on his back. I was told
afterwards that the Engineer Officer was a non-swimmer
and had been supported by the Captain all the time he was
in the water.

Much to our relief the enemy ship stopped firing her guns
but continued to circle us. Her Captain must have been a
very puzzled man. He could not have known what had happened to the submarine. He did not know if she had been
sunk or was still afloat, and she might even be lying at periscope depth waiting for an opportunity to attack his ship. I
began to wonder if he would stop his ship to pick us up and
what would happen if he did not. The coastline of Italy was
visible and I wondered if I could manage to swim there
should the necessity arise. I was fortunately a good swimmer
and, except for the oil fuel, I suffered no hardship. I was
expending little energy in keeping afloat and felt confident
that I would be able to do so for some considerable time.
Those of the crew who were wearing the Davis Apparatus
were supporting others who were without it. On one occasion I saw two men being supported by one man wearing
the gear. He had inflated the breathing bag to almost bursting point.

The destroyer had been circling us for about an hour
when she suddenly altered course and headed towards us. It

seemed as though our Captain was going to be proved right and she would stop to pick us up, but as suddenly as she had altered course towards us she altered course away again and continued circling. It was most disappointing. The manoeuvre was repeated about fifteen minutes later and after a further interval of fifteen minutes she altered course yet again and came towards us at a much slower speed. She stopped about 100 yards from us, and a voice hailed us in broken English asking who we were and how many of us were surviving. As we were unaware of any losses we replied that there were fifty-five of us – the complement of five officers and fifty men of the *Oswald*. The voice then told us that a boat would be lowered to pick us up and we were to hurry or be left behind.

The boat was lowered and we swam to meet it. As we reached her, her crew pulled us aboard and the boat then turned towards the ship where a gangway had been lowered. On climbing this gangway we were directed to the quarter-deck where we were placed under armed guard.

The roll was called and it was discovered that three of the crew were missing. It was a mystery how this had happened because everyone had got out of the submarine and if any man had been observed in distress in the water he would have been helped. One could only assume that the men had been lost immediately on taking to the water when everyone else was preoccupied with their own safety. It was very sad that these men had died but we were indeed fortunate that our losses were limited to this comparatively small number.

We presented a very sorry sight as we stood on the deck of the destroyer. None of us had worn much clothing when we abandoned the submarine and some, having shed what little they were wearing, were naked. The destroyer, which we discovered was Italian and named *Vivaldi*, did not carry reserve stocks of clothing to meet an emergency such as this, but her crew rallied round and provided us each with a jersey and a pair of trousers from their own personal kit. We were all covered in oil fuel; our hair and beards, which had grown long during the patrol, were thick with the stuff.

Many thoughts passed through my mind as I lay later that night gazing up at the stars. I thought first of my wife and twin daughters and wondered how soon it would be before they were informed of my misfortune, and when I would next see them. I was now a prisoner of war and I wondered where we were being taken and what treatment we could expect. I was not proud of my contribution to the war effort; so little had been achieved by the *Oswald* that I felt ashamed to have been taken prisoner of war so soon. Much more was expected of a submarine in those grim days. In the midst of my musings I fell asleep and it was dawn when I woke.

Most of my shipmates were already awake and having found the deck of the *Vivaldi* hard were standing about in groups. I joined the group where our Captain was, and during the ensuing conversation he was asked why the *Oswald* was delayed in sailing from Alexandria. Feeling, I suppose, that secrecy among us was no longer necessary he said that the *Oswald* was supposed to have relieved HM Submarine *Phoenix* in the Straits of Messina. When the change over was due a recall signal was sent to the *Phoenix* and her acknowledgment of the signal would have been the signal for the *Oswald* to depart. Unfortunately there was no response, and as there was the possibility that her wireless was out of action and being repaired the signal was repeated at pre-arranged times for a whole week. As there was still no response it was assumed that she had been sunk, which indeed she had. The *Oswald* was then dispatched to take her place. I was very upset to hear of her loss because I had known her in China and had some very good friends in her crew.

Keeping close inshore the *Vivaldi* pressed on and in the early afternoon a number of warships were sighted, lying at anchor in a big bay. The voice that had hailed us originally belonged to one of the destroyer's officers and he came to the quarterdeck and ordered us below. We were taken to the Steerage Compartment where we caught an occasional glimpse of what was happening through the portholes. The destroyer was soon steaming through the lines of anchored warships and as she passed each one she received a thunderous cheer from the crews assembled on deck. She had achieved fame in having sunk an enemy submarine and was being received into the port in a manner befitting her renown.

When the last of the warships had paid homage, we were all ordered on deck again, the destroyer was moored, and so it was that on that afternoon of 1 August, 1940, the crew of the *Oswald* were the first prisoners of war to be landed in Italy.

A party of armed soldiers was waiting at the jetty and, on being handed over to them, we were marched to two waiting motor coaches. On clearing the docks we found ourselves in a fairly large town. The streets were lined with hundreds of cheering people and, except for a group of students who shook their fists at us, no signs of anger were apparent.

On leaving the *Vivaldi* we had lost our only means of communication, because the officer who had hailed us in the water was the only one we had met who could speak English. Orders henceforth were given by signs.

The coaches stopped outside some big double doors and we were marched through into a fairly large yard enclosed by a high wall. We were marched in single file around this wall and halted at one yard intervals from one another. Signs were then made for us to turn and face the wall and keep silent and I remember thinking to myself 'My word, we are going to be shot'. That was not to be our fate, however, because after about thirty minutes cars were heard outside the gates and signs were made for us to turn around and stand to attention. So we witnessed the entry into the yard of an Italian General and a number of other high-ranking officers. The General called for the *Capitano*, and our

Captain stepped forward to meet him. There then followed a discussion between the Italian officers.

The General and his retinue finally departed and signs were made for us to march through a door into the building. As we did so we were greeted by a group of nuns standing just inside the door. They each wore a beautiful smile and it was indeed a pleasure to meet them on that sad and miserable day. We were led into a hospital ward and to undress and get into bed. Up to that time I had not realized how tired I really was and as soon as my head touched the pillow I fell into a deep sleep. The events of the past sixteen hours had taken their toll.

We all slept for twenty-four hours and when we awoke we found that a dressing gown, a towel and a cake of soap had been placed beside each of our beds. The nuns, who were the nurses, then directed us to the bathroom where each had a badly-needed hot bath. Feeling much refreshed we returned to the ward where we observed that the bedding had been changed and we were once again ordered to get into bed. The nuns then brought us some food and when that had been disposed of a number of barbers came into the ward and gave each of us a hair cut and shave. We had no idea where we were but one of the barbers, who could speak a little English, told us that we were in the hospital of the Italian Naval Base at Taranto.

We remained in the hospital for three days and were then moved to one of the many barracks in the base where we were each issued with a complete new Italian sailor's uniform. Our Captain anticipated an interrogation and warned us to be very careful what we said. Except where it was to our advantage to speak the truth he advised us to give false answers to all questions.

It began the next day and we were interrogated singly in descending order of seniority. After questioning we were taken to another building without coming into contact with those waiting. When my turn arrived I was escorted to the office where there were two civilians seated at a desk and the reception that I received was totally unexpected. I was bidden 'Good morning', invited to take a seat and offered a cigarette. This, I thought, was not going to be too bad after all. Both the interrogators could speak perfect English and while one put the questions, the other took notes. I was first asked my name, address and rank, to which I answered truthfully. I knew that this information would be forwarded to the British Government, informing them of my capture and they, in turn, would inform my wife. There then followed a series of questions relating to the movements of the submarine since the outbreak of war. The interrogator appeared most anxious to know how long she had been operating in the Straits of Messina and if I knew of other submarines operating there. I was asked where she was on particular dates, how many actions in which she took part, and how many torpedoes she had fired. I found it difficult to give false answers to the questions and became a little confused. In answer to a question relating to the whereabouts of the submarine on a particular date, the interrogator found it necessary to remind me that in answer to a previous question as to her whereabouts on the previous day I had told him that she was at a place one thousand miles away. He asked me if she was fitted with wings and capable of flying one thousand miles in twenty-four hours!

The interrogator knew that I was giving spurious answers, as he must have known other members of the crew were, but perhaps some of us unintentionally gave him little bits of information, which, when put together gave him a fuller picture of our movements.

My interrogation was brought to a close by the Interrogator disclosing that he was a submarine expert of the Italian Navy and that during the 1914–18 war he had been attached to our Royal Navy as a Liaison Officer. It may be that after fighting with us during that period he found it sad to now be our enemy which, perhaps, explains his friendly approach to the interrogation. The cigarette that I had been given was the first I had smoked for four days.

The treatment we received was not as bad as we expected. We thought there would be reprisals for having sunk the troopship but as yet there were no signs. Our guards were friendly and did not interfere with us at all. They seemed most uncomfortable in the handling of their rifles and gave me the impression that they would have felt more at ease had they been strumming a mandolin and singing Neapolitan love songs. We were naturally anxious to write to our homes and when we requested facilities for doing so we were told that we had to wait. It appeared that arrangements for the reception of prisoners of war had not been completed and no one knew just what we were entitled to.

On the tenth day of our stay we were told to be ready to move early on the morning of the next day. We had no packing to do because we were wearing all our possessions and early the next morning the same two coaches that had brought us to the Base arrived to take us away. We were taken to a railway station where we boarded a train, which we managed to deduce with our limited Italian was bound for Venice. The journey, which took twenty-four hours, took us through the Apennines, and I remember thinking how beautiful the scenery was – a view I did not hold when I passed through the mountains on a later occasion! I fell asleep during the night and on the few occasions that I awoke I discovered our guards to be asleep as well. One of them was using my shoulder as a pillow. Thoughts of escape crossed my mind but were soon banished when I observed the passengers in the corridor glaring angrily at me. Had I made any attempt to escape they would have been only too pleased to betray me.

Arriving at Venice early the following morning we were marched from the station to the waterfront where we boarded a motor launch that took us to a small island situated a short distance from the mainland. Waiting on the jetty to receive us was a reception committee comprising an

Army Captain and Lieutenant, a Sergeant Major and about thirty soldiers. Our guards then handed us over and departed in the launch. The Army Captain introduced himself to our Captain as being the Commandant of the camp and they discovered, to their mutual advantage, that they could both speak French. Henceforth communication was no problem.

The island, named Poveglia, was really a quarantine station but had been turned into a temporary prisoner-of-war camp to accommodate us until a permanent camp could be got ready. Our capture and arrival in Italy so early in their entry into the war had apparently been an embarrassment to the Italian Government because no camps were ready.

The Commandant was a friendly type and he told us that he hoped we would cause him no trouble because he wanted to make life as pleasant as he possibly could for us. We were to be confined in the largest of the many buildings on the island and would be allowed out for exercise for periods of one hour in the mornings and one hour in the afternoons. The officers would receive pay equal to their corresponding rank in the Italian Army but the men would receive nothing. This was considered unfair but such were the orders of the Italian Government. When the Commandant had finished, we were marched to the building that we were to occupy. It was a large single-storey building surrounded by iron railings ten feet high. The interior was very clean and the accommodation was luxurious by comparison with the *Oswald*!

During the first night on the island, eight of us decided to escape. We had noticed that there were two guards patrolling the building outside the railings who frequently stopped, when they met, to have a chat. Our plan was to wait for one of these occasions and, by climbing through a window and scaling the railings on their blind side, get clear of the building. We were to then split up into pairs and find our own way off the island. My companion was to be a young member of the crew, whose name was Ron, with whom I had swum away from the *Oswald*.

On our way through the island in the morning we had crossed a small bridge spanning a creek where I had seen a small boat moored. I meant to take this boat and make for the open sea where there was the possibility that Ron and I might be picked up by a neutral ship or possibly by one of our own warships in that area.

Escape from the building proved surprisingly easy, but when Ron and I reached the boat we were dismayed to find that the oars were secured by a padlock and chain. Our plan, such as it was, had misfired and there was nothing more to do except return to the building. In no time we were once again back with our shipmates. We were followed closely by two more pairs who said that they had returned because they had seen other guards patrolling the island who would be difficult to evade. It was anticipated that the last pair would also return and sure enough they appeared the following morning. They, however, were covered from head to foot in mud and told us that, by swimming and wading, they had reached the mainland but had been arrested by the police and taken into custody. Due to the language difficulty it had been some time before they were able to convince the police of their identity and a message was then sent to the Commandant of the camp asking him to send an escort to collect two of his prisoners – which was the first he knew of their escape!

It had been a stupid venture, doomed to failure from the start. We were to discover that there was more to an escape than just breaking out of a camp; the problems really started once you were out and on your own. The result of our escapade was that our exercise period outside the building was summarily suspended, and more guards were posted to the camp. This was a good thing really because it meant that less soldiers would be available to send to the fighting fronts.

We had been on the island for about a week when two

36

civilians arrived, bringing with them a radio recording unit, and they invited any of us who wished to do so to make a record to be broadcast by the Italian Broadcasting Company to our families on their English news programme which went out every evening at six o'clock. We sought the advice of our Captain who, warned us that anyone making a record could quite well be charged with treason on his return to England but, despite this, two members of the crew did co-operate and a short time afterwards a radio set was installed in the building to enable us to listen to the actual broadcast. The records went out with no deletions, and one of the men gave a full account of events leading up to our being taken prisoners of war, gave the names of the three men that had been lost, and assured everyone that the rest of us were in perfect health, as indeed we were. The other man, who had been married a short time before leaving England, spoke chiefly to his wife but gave information which was of interest to other men's wives. My wife, for instance, who up to that time only knew that my submarine had been sunk, found out that I was very much alive and where I was being held prisoner of war, which was of great comfort to her.

The radio set was removed immediately after the broadcast and life proceeded in the same monotonous way as before. There was absolutely nothing to do. We had no books or newspapers to read and no games to play. We were still not allowed to write letters and there was no cup of tea or cigarette to look forward to. Our confinement to the building was relaxed after a few days when we were allowed out for one hour in the mornings and one hour in the afternoons and, finally, for the complete day.

Life became less tedious some few days later, when we were allowed to write short postcards to our families. We were also told that the Italian Government had decided to issue us with five cigarettes per man per day. That, indeed, was a red letter day. We had been on the island for a month when we were told to be ready to move at six o'clock on the following morning. We were being moved to a girls' school that was being used as a temporary prisoner-of-war camp — a most satisfactory arrangement!

Our departure from the island was vastly different from our arrival because when the guards came to collect us for the journey they brought with them bundles of handcuffs with which they handcuffed us in pairs. On boarding the launch to take us to the mainland we had to descend a companion-way into a saloon. Standing at the top was a Sergeant Major and as we descended he gave each of us a kick in our backsides. When we turned to retaliate he patted a revolver, which he wore strapped to his waist, indicating that if we tried anything he would shoot. On our arrival on the mainland we were marched to the railway station where we boarded a train and were soon on our way.

My companion, sharing my handcuffs, was Ron. On finding our handcuffs irksome, we removed them by slipping them down over our hands and placed them on the seat between us ready to slip on again should the necessity arise. In view of the escape, we were now considered to be dangerous characters and had more guards than on our previous journey. The train travelled all day through flat country and as darkness began to set in it began to climb into the Apennines. No food had been provided on the journey and we all began to feel hungry. Snow was lying deep on the ground and we also began to feel cold. Near midnight the train stopped at a station and we were told to get out. This was Sulmona and waiting for us were a number of army lorries, into which we were transfered and driven to our new camp in the mountains. There our particulars were taken and officers and men were separated and marched away to their respective buildings.

I cannot remember much of that march because black-out restrictions were in operation and we could see very little of our surroundings. I do recall passing through doors in very high walls, and we were finally ordered to halt outside a barn-like building and told to enter. By now some of us had picked up a few words of Italian and we asked our guards when we were likely to get any food, but they said they did not know. On being left to our own resources we groped around until we located beds. Feeling tired, cold and hungry, we lost no time in getting into bed and we were soon fast asleep.

On waking at daybreak we discovered that we were in a very large hut with white-washed walls, a corrugated roof and a concrete floor. There were ten other such huts in the compound. The prisoner-of-war camp, as indeed it was, was situated on sloping ground in a valley high in the foothills of the Apennines and on looking down from the highest point of our compound we could see that the camp comprised a number of these compounds, the whole being encircled by a double barbed wire fence about fifteen feet high. Situated on the outside of the fence were a number of elevated sentry boxes manned by armed sentries. A more bleak and desolate scene was hard to envisage, ill befitting its name of Fonte Di Amore, or Valley Of Love. The camp, we were told, had been used as a prisoner-of-war camp in the First World War and had been lying derelict since that period. Adjoining the camp was a Penal Establishment similar to our Dartmoor and we often saw the prisoners outside the prison cracking stones.

The crew of the *Oswald* were the first prisoners to arrive in the camp but it was not long before other prisoners from North Africa began to arrive. They were of mixed nationality; besides English, Irish, Scots and Welsh, there were Australians, New Zealanders, Tasmanians and Sikhs and a fine crowd of men they were too. They were nearly all soldiers but there were a few of the RAF among them, and the camp was soon filled.

The Commandant was a Colonel of the *Carabinieri* (Colonel of Police) and the guards were a mixture of police and soldiers. They did not interfere unduly and left the internal organization of the camp to us. The coxswain of the *Oswald*, who was the senior in rank, became camp leader. There was not a lot for him to do, but he maintained some sort of order in the camp, and acted as our spokesman and also took the blame for any misdemeanours committed by the prisoners.

Our food was supplied raw and was cooked by a few of the prisoners in a very primitive cookhouse. Our rations consisted only of macaroni, tomato paste, a small piece of fat pork for frying purposes, and vegetables – rotten swedes and pumpkins. In addition each man received a small loaf of bread made from maize flour each day. On rare occasions, when there was a surplus of macaroni, it was crushed into flour and each man received a pancake. We were supposed to receive the same rations as an Italian soldier and if he had to fight on those rations he had my sympathy.

The washing and toilet facilities were of a very primitive nature. The bathroom was an open shed in which there were a couple of cold water taps and when taking a bath one had to stand on the concrete floor, in all winds and weathers, and wash down in cold water. In winter it was really cold. The lavatory was in another shed and this consisted of a number of holes in the floor over which one had to squat.

There were no language problems in this camp because we had two interpreters, one a Second Lieutenant, the other a Sergeant-Major. Having both worked in London prior to the war they spoke excellent English. They differed in one respect: the officer was anti-British, while the Sergeant-Major was pro-British. It was the duty of these interpreters to call the roll twice daily – at eight am and again at five pm. In extremely bad weather the Sergeant-Major would perform this duty while we remained in bed, but the officer would have us parade outdoors and would delight in keeping us as long as possible.

We had been in the camp for about a month when mail from home began to arrive. One or two letters per day arrived at first and then it began to arrive by the sackful. I cannot really describe my feelings at receiving my first letter from my wife; it was certainly one of the happiest moments of my life. Shortly after the arrival of the letters, parcels began to come through. They contained articles of clothing, books, cigarettes: all sent from our homes. We also received Red Cross food parcels without which I am sure many of us would have died. They proved to be our salvation for the Italian rations were totally inadequate and as the war progressed they grew steadily worse. The contents of these parcels varied a little, but a typical example would be – a half-pound tin of butter or margarine, a packet of tea, coffee or cocoa, a packet of sugar, a tin of meat loaf, a packet of biscuits, a bar of chocolate, a tin of Marmite or Oxo cubes, a tin of jam or honey, a packet of prunes or raisins, a tin of pilchards, and a bar of soap. They also sent cigarettes and we each received a weekly issue of fifty.

Following the food parcels, bales of clothing, also sent by the Red Cross Society, arrived in the camp. There were battledress suits, overcoats, pullovers, shirts, underclothes, boots and socks, and we each received a complete outfit.

It has been said that adversity brings out all that is good or bad in a man and I could not agree more with that observation. I discovered that there is a little bad in the best of us and a little good in the worst. It was sad to observe men of hitherto sound principles suddenly develop bad streaks and yet on the other hand it was heartening to observe men who previously had been of unprincipled nature suddenly become possessed of many admirable qualities. I discovered that I had developed an urge to assist those less fortunate than myself. I considered myself fortunate because at the time of my capture I had been a regular member of the Royal Navy for thirteen and a half years and, as I had been looking after myself for the whole of that period, it was no hardship for me to have to continue to do so as a prisoner of war. Similarly, I was able to help others less accustomed to fending for themselves. When anyone received bad news from home and had to tell someone about it, I was prepared to listen. Sometimes I was able to offer advice or comfort, but it was best just to listen. I found that if a man was troubled, it was best to let him talk and unburden himself.

We managed to procure an old piano from our guards and on deciding to put on a variety show we invited the Commandant to attend on the opening night. The show was opened by the singing of our National Anthem and he was expected to stand to attention. This proved too much of an embarrassment to him and he stamped out in a rage and refused to attend any further functions.

A few weeks before Christmas we received a visit from a very high dignitary of the Vatican. He brought us the Pope's blessing and his best wishes for a Happy Christmas, hoping that we would soon be reunited with our families. He also brought us each a small present of a packet of twenty cigarettes and a packet of cocoa. That visit became an annual event and was very much appreciated.

It was shortly after Christmas that the first escape from this camp was attempted. Two soldiers were involved and they succeeded in getting out of the camp but were caught shortly afterwards. There were a number of civilians working in our compound and these two soldiers evolved a plan to mingle with them as they left work one afternoon and walk out of the camp. Their first essential was a civilian suit and this was obtained by collecting all the odd bits of material that they could and sewing them together and then cutting them into the various panels required to make suits. It was a long job because everything had to be done by hand, but they were finally completed and although not quite up to Savile Row standard they served the purpose. A dye then had to be obtained and this was done by asking everyone in the camp to take the paper labels from the tins in their Red Cross food parcels and put them in a bucket of water which was then boiled, thereby extracting the printers' ink. The resulting dye was a colour the like of which I had not seen before but that, too, served its purpose.

On the day chosen for the escape the two soldiers donned their suits and waited in a hut near the gates of the compound. A helper was standing opposite the hut and he kept the two informed, by signs, of what was happening. As the workmen passed the hut they slipped out and joined them at the rear. They passed the sentry at the gates and got clear of the camp but as they were walking along the road one of the workmen happened to look back and observing that they had strangers in their midst, ran back to the camp and raised the alarm. So ending their escape bid. They were brought back to the camp and after a severe beating were placed in the cells in the guards' quarters where they remained, in solitary confinement, for thirty days.

The duty officer happened to be our Lieutenant interpreter, whom we had named Alberto, and he came charging into the compound followed by about twenty of the guards. Being the duty officer he would be held responsible for the escape, and he was consequently in a tearing rage. He ordered everyone to parade in the middle of the compound and the guards then made a search of the huts looking for any escape material. This was a classic example of locking the stable door after the horse had gone. Other prospective escapees had long since buried their material in the ground.

The search lasted for about an hour, without anything being discovered, which made Alberto even more angry. He walked up and down in front of us, ranting and raving, and calling us all the names on which he could lay his tongue. This did not trouble us at all but when he challenged any of us to step forward and fight him, it proved too much for an army corporal standing near me and he stepped forward to take up the challenge. As he did so the guards clubbed him to the ground with the butt end of their rifles and continued to beat him as he lay on the ground. We all surged forward to go to his assistance and as we did so Alberto fired his revolver into the air and threatened to order the guards to shoot if we did not go back. We had no alternative but to obey and when order was finally restored we were dismissed. On returning to our huts we were faced with a scene of such chaos that it seemed as if a tornado had swept through the camp. All our personal belongings were scattered all over the

43

floor including the contents of our food parcels. It was a heartbreaking sight.

It was some time before we sorted things out, but henceforth these searches became a common occurrence and we got used to them. No warning was given when a search was about to take place. We were ordered to parade as if for roll call and then the guards would disappear into our huts and start foraging. The odd part about these searches was that the prisoners themselves were never searched, so if anyone was in possession of any escape material they could quite safely carry it with them as an alternative to burying it. Photographs and letters could also be carried. There was always a plan to escape being put into operation but during the time that I was in this camp none were successful.

If an attempt at escape failed, it was not fruitless because of its nuisance value. The guards and their officers were kept continually on the alert and in some instances extra guards were drafted to the camp. This meant that there was that less number to fight against our troops in the battlefields.

Despite having neither newspapers nor radio, news seeped into the camp in many mysterious ways and we were thus able to follow the course of the war. It was a very sad day indeed when our guards came charging into the compound and told us that HMS *Hood* had been sunk. To us of the Royal Navy this seemed unbelievable. The *Hood* was a household name in England, a great morale booster and the pride of the Royal Navy.

The officers' compound adjoined ours, with a dividing wall about 20 feet high, and when any news was received in either compound it was written on a piece of paper, wrapped around a stone and thrown over the wall where there would always be someone to pick it up and spread the information around. I remember one occasion when I was standing near this wall one of these missiles came sailing over and hit my head. When I peeled off the paper, in place of a stone was a jar of ointment for the treatment of haemorrhoids and the message was from the Captain of the *Oswald* instructing the finder to pass on the ointment to a named member of his crew. I threw a message back asking him if he had anything for the cure of a headache that his jar of ointment had given me.

The Italians did not worry us unduly. The only time that we saw them was for roll-call and when a search took place. There were times, however, when one of the prisoners committed an offence and had to be punished. The most common offence was leaving escape material among one's belongings which was discovered by the guards during a search. Punishment consisted of being confined in cells in the guards' quarters by night, and during the day, regardless of the state of the weather, the offender would be handcuffed with his arms around a telegraph post. The periods of punishment varied but the most usual was thirty days.

I had been in this camp for about eighteen months when instructions were given to the camp leader to select twenty men to go to another camp to prepare it for the arrival of officer prisoners from North Africa. On the arrival of the officers, the men were to remain as batmen. I did not like the idea of becoming a batman, but it did provide an opportunity to get away from the camp. Both Ron and I volunteered to be included in this party. We were selected without any difficulty because the coxswain of the *Oswald* was camp leader and with eight more of our shipmates and ten soldiers we were instructed to be ready to move off on the afternoon of the next day.

III. THE CASTLE

Our journey once again took us by rail through the mountains but as night began to fall we passed into flat country. At 1 am we changed trains at Rome for Piacenza and then were driven by coach to the village of Rezzanello and the castle there that was our destination.

There was a welcoming committee of five Italian officers: a Colonel, a Major, a Captain and two Lieutenants. The Colonel was the Camp Commandant, the Major was the doctor, the Captain, who was in the Alpine Regiment and wore an alpine hat with a feather in it, was the second in command. Of the two Lieutenants, one was in charge of the guards and the other was the interpreter. The latter, whose name was Prevadini, then addressed us. He spoke perfect English and had many English mannerisms. He told us why we were at the camp, and warned us that anyone caught in the act of escaping would be shot. We were standing outside the castle near a number of huts which was the administrative section of the camp and also the guards' quarters. Prevadini showed us where the cells were if anyone misbehaved. He finally said all he had to and we were then marched into the castle and conducted to our quarters. We were told that we would be free for the rest of the day and would be required for work the following morning.

Our quarters were in the basement of the castle and the first thing we noticed was a number of sacks of straw lying on the floor which were to be our beds. The floor was stone and very damp. There were windows, about two foot square, and when we looked out of them we had to look up to see daylight because we were below ground level.

At least we did not have to wait to be fed because we all had our food parcels. After a sleep we all had a meal. Some of the guards saw our food and their eyes nearly popped out of their heads. They were experiencing very severe food rationing and had forgotten that food, such as ours, existed.

The castle itself was oblong in shape with four wings each about 40 feet wide and a courtyard in the middle. One each corner were turrets surmounted by pinnacles which rose above the roof. The interior consisted of rooms of varying sizes and the ceilings and walls of most of them were covered with paintings of religious subjects. It stood in beautiful grounds with masses of flowers growing in well-kept flower beds. We were told that the castle was owned by a Scotsman who, on the outbreak of war, had returned to Scotland and it had then been taken over by the Italian Government to be used as a prisoner-of-war camp.

There were two entrances to the castle and we were told that while the front entrance was out of bounds we could leave by the rear entrance to walk in the grounds. A gravel path surrounded the castle along which we exercised and outside this was the usual double barbed wire fence with the customary elevated sentry boxes manned by the inevitable armed sentries – a most depressing sight. It was situated high in the mountains and commanded a good view of the town of Piacenza and also the Plains of Lombardy which stretched far into the distance. It was summer time and the corn growing in the surrounding fields had ripened so that it seemed as though a huge golden carpet had been laid on the ground. It was a scene so tranquil and sublime that one was reminded of one's own beloved English countryside. We were informed that we would be allowed in the grounds from 8 am to 6 pm each day. During the forbidden period the gates would be locked and anyone then found outside would be shot.

We were up and about early on the following morning and were soon hard at work preparing the rooms for the arrival of the officers. The task was finished in three days,

47

and we then had three days rest before the arrival of the officers. There were 150 of them, mostly Army men, plus a few from the Royal Navy and a few from the RAF. The senior officer was a Brigadier and the others were of varying ranks down to Second Lieutenant. They were in a very sorry plight because they had just come from the battle-fields of North Africa and their sole possessions were the clothes they were wearing. As this was a newly established camp, supplies of clothing and food had not yet been sent from England, but it was not long before they started to come through.

In the allocation of duties as batmen five of my shipmates and I were appointed cleaners and disposers of refuse. Our job was to keep clean that part of the castle not occupied by the officers, and to dispose of all rubbish daily. The other men looked after the officers and their quarters. The officers received pay from the Italians and in turn they paid us for our services. There was a canteen in the castle, run by the Italians, and although we did not receive a lot of money, and did not expect a lot, we were able to make small purchases which made life a little more pleasant. We complained to the Brigadier about our beds and quarters, and after he had made an inspection he decided that the conditions were un-satisfactory and strode off to complain to the Commandant. As a consequence we were moved to the attic of the castle and provided with proper beds and bedding. We did not have the bedding for long, however, because our sheets were collected and not returned, and we were told that this was a reprisal for the Italian prisoners of war in England having had their sheets taken away.

Although the Italian army doctor came into the castle every day to attend at his surgery, he was not really required because amongst our own officers there were six doctors of the RAMC and they looked after our health. The Italian doctor was very pro-British, however, and every day he would tell our medical orderly the news, who would then write it on a piece of paper to be read to everyone when they were all together. When it had been read to everyone the paper would then be destroyed.

We unfortunately did not have a dentist and for treatment had to rely on the service of an Italian army dentist, also a Major, who visited the camp once a month. Shortly after one of his visits I developed a bad toothache and had to wait over three weeks for his next visit when I presented myself at the surgery. I joined thirty other patients, officers and men, in the waiting room. The first patient was a shipmate of mine and he came back to the waiting room holding his jaw, and told us that the dentist had extracted one of his teeth without using an anaesthetic! Everyone, with the exception of myself, then made a mad dash to get out of the room. They dived out of the door and window and I had never seen a room vacated so quickly. I sat there pondering the situation and I decided that the pain to be endured by having the offending tooth extracted could be no worse than the pain that I was already enduring, so I entered the surgery. I was invited by the dentist to sit in the chair and as I did so two Italian medical orderlies pounced on me and pinioned my arms to the arms of the chair. The dentist then approached me from behind and opening my mouth inserted an instrument which I thought was a prober, but was really his extractors. He had no difficulty in locating the offending tooth and soon had it out. The operation only lasted a few seconds, but while it was going on I had the feeling that the top of my head was being lifted off. With a 'bravo' and a pat on the back from the dentist I then left the surgery. The news that two of the crew of the *Oswald* had had teeth extracted without an anaesthetic soon spread through the castle and it was generally accepted that we submariners could certainly take it.

At that time (1942) there was a shortage not only of anaesthetics, but of medical supplies in general. The Italian doctor told us that the demand from hospitals and from the battlefields far exceeded the supply. He also told us that amputations of limbs were being performed without

49

anaesthetics, so I could not complain at having one wretched tooth extracted without one.

Day after day and week after week, life in the castle proceeded in the same monotonous way. We would wake up in the morning to face a day the same as yesterday and the day before and the day before that. A general feeling of boredom and lethargy prevailed, but on occasions there was a little variety introduced into the daily routine when attempts to escape took place. When an attempt did take place it was as much a surprise to those of the prisoners not taking part as it was to the Italians. It had to be approached with the utmost secrecy because there was the possibility that there might be informers in the castle amongst our own men, as not all prisoners of war were escape-minded. There were some, who, having been taken prisoner were happy in the knowledge that they were safe, and were no longer to take an active part in the war, and were quite content to languish in a prisoner-of-war camp, without causing any trouble to the Italians, and just wait for the war to end. Of these there were some who considered it a nuisance when an attempt was foiled and collective punishment imposed, and it was amongst these few that informers were most likely to be found. One of these characters was under suspicion but we could prove nothing against him. I did not agree with collective punishment being imposed for one man's attempt to escape, but it was all part of the game and had to be accepted. I admired any man who was escape minded and was prepared to assist him in any way I could, and when the opportunity arose to have a go myself.

The first attempt in this camp was made by a Colonel of the Royal Engineers and although he worked at it in full view of everyone in the camp, and sometimes the Italians, very few knew what he was doing. There was a gravel path encircling the castle and close to it was the barbed wire fence – the whole not being more than 30 feet from the castle walls. The Colonel had asked the Commandant to extend the fence further into the grounds in order that he could grow vegetables. This request was approved and I remember thinking what an awful shame it was to dig into ground that was so pleasing to the eye.

With one helper the Colonel then started to prepare the land for his vegetables and when he chose to grow tomatoes we all thought that he had become mentally ill because they were both plentiful and cheap. He, however, had other plans. He meant to dig a tunnel under the wire and use the tomato plants, when fully grown, as a shield for his activities. In digging a tunnel in a prisoner-of-war camp, the main problem is the disposal of earth dug out. The Colonel did not have to overcome that problem because part of his allotment was always newly dug and would therefore not arouse suspicion when earth from the tunnel was scattered over it. The gardening tools were on loan from the Italians and had to be returned to them every evening when the gates were closed, to ensure that they were not used for any other purpose. It was arranged by the Colonel and his helper that only one would work in the tunnel while the other remained on top pottering around and keeping a look-out, ready to give warning of approaching danger; he would also pull up the soil excavated from the tunnel and scatter it around. When they ceased work for the day they would place twigs across the top of the shaft, on top of which they would place turves to conceal it from prying eyes.

One of the duties of the sergeant of the guard was to call everyone in from the grounds and, after he had made a search, to lock the gate. We, who knew of the Colonel's activities, would watch him from one of the windows of the castle hoping that he would not discover the tunnel. He would seldom go near the allotment, but he did so one evening – more to admire the tomatoes than anything else, I think – and, stepping on the turves, he disappeared into the tunnel. Serious as it was for the Colonel, I do not think that I have laughed so much in all my life. It was so funny – one minute the sergeant was in full view and the next he had disappeared completely. It was with difficulty that he managed to climb out of the hole and he then lost no time in dashing off to report his discovery to the Commandant. That worthy gentleman came charging into the castle at the head of his guards, brandishing his revolver and screaming like a madman. Everyone was ordered to parade and the usual search of the castle commenced. That was the end of the Colonel's escape bid and the start of thirty days solitary confinement in the cells. Collective punishment was then imposed and everyone was confined to the castle for one week and the barbed wire fence was returned to its original position with a complete ban on the future cultivation of tomatoes!

To those contemplating an escape, as I and two comrades were at that time, the prospects did not appear to be very bright. With barbed wire fences encircling the camp, floodlit at night, and with the armed sentries in their sentry boxes, escape seemed an impossibility, but there was a way out and sooner or later it would be found. Sometimes it would come by prolonged thought and sometimes it would reveal itself when least expected. It was least expected when a way out revealed itself to me.

The duties of the rubbish disposal squad involved the collection of the rubbish from the castle and after placing it in a hand cart they would present themselves at the front gate of the castle where one of the guards would be waiting to escort them about 200 yards down the drive to a rubbish dump. This duty would be performed once daily, usually at 11 am, and it was while returning from one of these excursions that the seeds of a plan were sown.

The castle had three floors and each floor led into the turrets. All windows were barred and there were shutters provided which had to be closed at night. Escape via the windows was therefore impossible, or considered by the Italians to be impossible, until I happened to glance up at the turrets and observed that the window on the attic floor where the batmen had their quarters was not barred. How I had missed noticing that on the previous occasions that I had been outside the castle I do not know, but there it was: the weak link in the chain.

I knew that the doorway leading into the turret from the attic was bricked up but that presented no problem because bricks can be removed. The fact that the guards' quarters were immediately under the window did not present a problem either because I felt that the boldest of plans was the most likely to succeed.

On returning to the castle I sought out my comrade, Ron, and told him of my discovery. On asking him if he would consider escaping with me, he thought that I was joking, but when he realized I was in earnest he told me that I was mad. He nevertheless agreed to accompany me and became as enthusiastic as I was. Before making a final decision, however, we both agreed that we first of all had to find out if conditions outside that part of the castle favoured a night escape bid.

It so happened that one of our comrades, a soldier nicknamed Paddy, was serving a five days' sentence in the cells in the guards' quarters for being late on roll-call and it was to him that we looked for the information that we required. His food had to be taken to him by one of his comrades and as lunch time was approaching I offered to do it. The guard at the gate let me out and after unlocking the door of Paddy's cell, which was about fifteen feet from the gate, allowed me to enter unaccompanied while he returned to his post at the gate. I was thus able to tell Paddy of my plan to escape and asked him for his co-operation in obtaining the information that was required. He agreed to co-operate on condition that he, too, was included in the plan. I had no objection to this, so I told him we needed to know the number of guards on duty and their habits, the number of lights burning and their position, and if the officer of the guard or the sergeant of the guard made any rounds. I then left him to return to the castle to await his release.

He reported that conditions at night were very favourable. He said that off duty guards retired to their quarters each night leaving only one on duty at the gates. Blackout restrictions were in operation and there was only one very feeble light situated above the gate casting its rays downwards. That part of the castle at the foot of the turret was in complete darkness and with the sentry on his post at the gate we could not be seen. As regards the sentry, luck favoured us because when things quietened down in the castle he would pop into a hut nearby, perhaps to have a smoke or sit down, and would occasionally put his head out to have a look around. The duty officer was never seen but the duty sergeant made the rounds of all sentry posts every two hours, starting at ten o'clock. It was apparent that escape from that part of the castle was not anticipated by the Italians, hence the poor security measures. However, it was the unexpected that often succeeded.

Our plan was to cut a hole in the bricked-up doorway leading into the turret, climb out of the window and down a rope to the ground. After escaping we would climb further into the mountains and then head north to Switzerland and freedom. It is all so easy to put down on paper but when it comes to putting it into practice it is a different matter altogether. Tools and a rope were required, and those are things that are not normally left lying around in a prisoner-of-war camp. The method employed in cutting through the wall had to be noiseless as any undue sound would have alerted the guards. We chose as our tools table knives and the handles of table forks and spoons, which were sharpened by rubbing them up and down the stone walls of the castle. The bricks of the wall were of the red clay type, laid with mortar, and our plan was to scrape the mortar surrounding one of the bricks and remove it. This would make the removal of sufficient of the other bricks a lot easier. The mess could be disposed of on my daily excursions to the rubbish dump with the camp refuse.

Our Red Cross food parcels were contained in cardboard boxes which, in turn, were secured with string and it was this string that I used to make the rope. Once again my job as refuse collector stood me in good stead because I was able to salvage string from the rubbish. When I undid the knots I was left with little bits of string, none longer than two feet. These lengths then had to be joined to make lengths of sixty feet. As it was a type of string that could not be spliced it had to be knotted and the twelve lengths then had to be divided into three sections of four lengths. These were then plaited to produce a rope sixty feet in length, strong enough to support a man's weight. During its manufacture I kept the rope, and unused material, under my mattress and I was indeed fortunate that no searches took place during that period.

A courageous man can be defined in many ways and one definition I call to mind is 'He who is afraid and yet goes forward'. It was aptly illustrated when, in the course of the rope's manufacture, I caught Ron gazing at it rather apprehensively. He knew that if the rope parted while he was climbing down it, he would possibly fall to his death but he nevertheless continued with the venture. I had no qualms about the strength of the rope and considered it strong enough not only to support one man but the combined weight of the three of us. With bits of string poking out from the knots it did not look very impressive, but its strength lay in the plaiting, and when it took the strain of a man's weight the strands bound each other and prevented slipping.

We worked only by day, Paddy or Ron digging the hole in the wall and I manufacturing the rope. We had fixed a clothes line to the wall above the hole and when danger threatened washed clothes were hung on it to conceal our activities. It was also left hanging there each night, and I had to stuff the rope under my mattress and lie on the bed to flatten it.

We had accumulated a stock of concentrated food such as Oxo and Marmite cubes, Ovaltine tablets and chocolate, which we thought would be sufficient to sustain us should we succeed in escaping and not be able to obtain other food. We tossed a coin to decide in which order the descent of the rope was to be made and it was to be Paddy first, me second and Ron third. As I was the only seaman of the three I had to instruct the other two in the art of climbing down a rope. I told them to cross their legs on the rope and when they started to descend to grip it tight with their knees and feet, so that by exerting, or relaxing, pressure they could regulate their speed of descent. I told them that on no account were they to allow the rope to slide through their hands because of rope burn, which I knew from past experience to be extremely painful and might cause them to let go of the rope.

On the night chosen for the escape zero hour was to be at 12.30 after the sergeant of the guard had completed his rounds of the sentries and was relaxing until his next visit at two o'clock. We hoped that it would also be at a time when the sentry at the gate had gone into his hut for a smoke. If we were successful in reaching the ground we were to walk away from the castle in a straight line, which would be on grass to the rear of the administrative buildings parallel to the drive, and to continue until we reached the rubbish dump where we were to rendezvous. From there we were to penetrate deeper into the mountains and head for Switzerland. We did not quite know what would happen if we did reach Switzerland. As it was a neutral country there was the possibility that we would be interned but there was also the possibility that we would be sent home. Whichever it was to be, it would be infinitely better than languishing in a prisoner-of-war camp.

The success of the venture depended on our being able to climb silently down the rope. I had no doubts about my own ability to do so, but I was a little dubious about my comrades – I would have felt happier if I had two of my seamen colleagues with me.

I had lashed four short lengths of broom handles ladder fashion, and the idea of this was to hang it out of the window with the top piece level with the outside edge of the window ledge so that when we dropped the rope out of the window it would ride over the top and prevent it from chafing when we put our weight on it. The other three lengths of wood hanging down would keep the rope away from the sides of the turret thereby making it easier to grip as we climbed out of the window. Part of the iron frame of a damaged bed was to be placed across the inside of the window to act as an anchor for the rope.

If the escape was successful one of our fellow prisoners had volunteered to pull the rope back into the turret where it was to be left. He was then to replace the bricks and conceal the hole. If it was not discovered, it would provide a way of escape for anyone else so inclined.

As zero hour approached on the night chosen for the escape, we assembled in the turret and after giving my mates final instructions on how to lower themselves down the rope I placed the four lengths of broom handle in position and lowered the rope. We wished each other the best of luck and Paddy then climbed on to the window ledge and lay on his stomach with his legs hanging outside. I told him to feel around for the rope with his feet and having located it to grip it with his legs as I had taught him. I then told him to lower himself a little until he could grip the rope with his hands and, having done that, he started to descend.

I watched him until he was engulfed by the darkness when he seemed to be going well but shortly afterwards I heard a noise as if he was scraping his boots on the side of the turret. This was followed by shouts in Italian and I knew that the attempt had failed. In some way or another, Paddy had bungled it but there was no time for Ron and I to bemoan our bad luck. We had to get undressed and into bed before the guards arrived. We threw our parcels of food out of the window and then climbed through the hole back to our quarters. It was futile to try to conceal the way of escape so the rope was left dangling out of the window and the bricks left lying around. Almost as soon as we started to undress we heard the sound of running feet in the courtyard below and knew that we would soon receive a visit from the guards. We just had time to get into bed before they arrived. They went straight to the hole and after finding no one in the turret they pulled the bedclothes from the beds of everyone sleeping in the attic. They knew that Paddy was not alone in the attempted escape and were looking for his accomplices who might be lying fully clothed in bed. They obviously did not find anyone but if they had felt our clothes, which were warm, they would have had us.

There then followed the usual parade in the courtyard followed by the roll call and search of the castle.

Very few of the prisoners knew of the escape attempt and, as no man is at his best on being awakened in the middle of the night to stand in the cold for a couple of hours, many harsh words were spoken. I heard one officer threaten to have Prevadini, who was duty officer, barred from returning to England to resume his job after the war. It so happened that the Commandant and his second-in-command were both on leave and Prevadini was also acting Commandant as well as being duty officer. It was not long before our rope and four pieces of wood were found and carried out of the castle in triumph. It was sad to think that all our hard work had come to nothing but I was more concerned about Paddy. All I knew about him was that he had been caught. I did not have a clue what had happened, but I was relieved not to have heard the sound of gunfire. The scraping of his boots on the side of the turret obviously meant that he was not gripping the rope with his legs which, in turn, meant that he was allowing the rope to slide through his hands and that, I knew, would give him rope burn. I was determined to find out how he was at the earliest possible moment which would be when I presented myself at the gates with his breakfast. A sentry had been left in the attic to guard the hole and at daybreak a bricklayer arrived to block it up and to fit bars to the window. Collective punishment was once again imposed, everyone being confined to the castle for one week.

Promptly at breakfast time I presented myself at the gates with Paddy's breakfast but I was not allowed through. The food was taken from me by one of the guards who took it into Paddy in the cells. That routine prevailed for three days until I was allowed into the cells accompanied by one of the guards who forbade me to speak. Paddy was looking well but when he held his hands out to take his food I could see that they were in bad shape with rope burn. He could not take his food. He had held his hands out purposely for me to see them and having done that he motioned me to put his food on his bed. I reported to one of our doctors what I had seen and he, exercising his right as a doctor, demanded immediate access to the cells and was thus able to treat Paddy. I shudder to think what pain he must have endured for those first three days.

He was sentenced to serve thirty days in the cell and Ron and I had to wait until his release to find out his story. He then told us that on starting to slide down the rope things had gone very well. He had followed my instructions and had been surprised at the ease with which he was descending, but after a while his trouser leg slipped up and he found himself gripping the rope with his bare legs. This became unbearable and he was forced to release his grip of the rope with his legs but, on transferring the whole of his weight to his arms, he found that they were not strong enough to allow him to continue descending hand over hand. He allowed the rope to slide through his hands. This then caused rope burn which forced him to release some of the pressure he was exerting on the rope and his speed of descent increased. To check this he scraped the sides of the turret with his boots, the noise that I heard, and succeeded in alerting the sentry.

On reaching the ground he ran towards the sentry who had emerged from the hut but who had forgotten to bring his rifle. Before he could go back to get it Paddy had wrapped his arms around him in surrender. He was extremely lucky because had the sentry been at his post he would not have hesitated to shoot. He had then been taken into the guardroom to be questioned. Among other things the Italians wanted to know who his accomplices were but he had not divulged that information. He said that he had not been ill-treated, but when he asked for treatment for his hands, which were in very bad shape and very painful he was told that as there were no medical supplies for the Italian soldiers there were none for him. He expressed regret for having bungled the escape, but I told him not to worry: there could always be another time.

The preparations for the escape had occupied our minds for a few weeks and relieved the boredom, and here we were now back at square one once again. However, the arrival of some more batmen shortly afterwards took our minds off things for a while. We could not understand why additional batmen had been sent to the castle. We had not been over-worked and had not asked for additional men, but the mystery was solved a short time later when all the officers were moved to another camp and were replaced by a greater number of South African officers. These officers were not so steeped in tradition as the English and were consequently more amiable and easier to get on with. I remember one in particular, Lieutenant 'Ginger' Hamilton, who became a very firm favourite with all the men.

It was shortly after their arrival that an incident occurred which implicated me in the escape attempt. The game of volley ball was very popular in the camp but the net had fallen into such a bad state of repair that I offered to make another one. String was required from the Red Cross food parcels so a request was made to the Commandant to grant me some. He agreed to the request with the proviso that it had to be weighed when issued and also at night when it had to be handed with the partly completed net to the duty officer to ensure that it was not used for escape purposes.

The string was of a suitable thickness to form the mesh of the net but the ridge rope, or frame, had to be much thicker so I made that by plaiting some lengths, as I had done in making the rope for the escape. It was soon completed and in use.

Occasionally when a game was in progress the Italian officers would come into the castle to watch, among them Prevadini. He knew that I had made the net and on spotting me among the spectators came over to me and congratulated me on a fine job. I blushed at such unexpected praise but my blushes quickly vanished when he pointed out the similarity between the net and the rope used in the escape. I was promptly accused of manufacturing it and marched to the cells to serve a fifteen days' sentence. It just shows how stupid one can be.

I was not alone in the cells because one of my fellow prisoners was already there for having cursed one of the guards. He was a regular soldier who had seen service on the North West Frontier of India and while serving there had studied Yoga. It was his practice to stand on his head in a corner of the cell for varying periods throughout the day in order to stimulate his mental faculties. My way to do that was to lie flat on my back on my bed and just gaze into space. We kept ourselves fit by doing physical exercises. In the evenings the guards off duty used to congregate outside the cells and, to the accompaniment of mandolins and guitars, they would sing the romantic songs of their country. I used to look forward to these sessions and, all in all, I spent an enjoyable fifteen days in the cells.

On my release I was classified by the Italians as an escaper and in ensuing searches my belongings came in for special attention.

The South African officers did not remain with us for long because they, too, were removed to another camp and were replaced by more English officers. We were moved much less frequently; perhaps the Italians considered the officers to be more valuable as prisoners than the men and were not prepared to take any risk of them escaping.

One of the batmen was a New Zealand soldier whom we knew as 'Kiwi'. He was about five feet four inches tall and weighed about ten stone, and was one of the toughest characters I have ever met. He was of a morose disposition and did not make friends easily, so I was surprised when he approached me one day and said that he would like to speak to me. It turned out that he contemplated escaping and asked for my help. I agreed to help him in any way I could and asked him how. He said that the idea for escape had only come to him that morning as he watched my mates and me leave the castle with the rubbish. His plan was for the rubbish disposal gang to put him in a sack, place it in the bottom of our cart covered in rubbish and then wheel it out of the castle to the rubbish dump where we were to leave him. I was dumbfounded and could not speak for a full two minutes. I had been racking my brains for months trying to think of a way of escape, and every day I had the means of escape in my hands! It was a simple but effective plan, and it surprised me that no one had thought of it before.

Our routine in disposing of the rubbish was to present ourselves at the front gates of the castle at 10 am when the sentry on duty would call two of his colleagues to escort us down the drive to the dump. We would never hurry on these excursions because it was a break from life inside the castle. We were familiar with all the guards and would chat and argue with them. It was also an opportunity to do a spot of bartering. It sometimes happened that we had surplus articles from our Red Cross food parcels which we were able to swap with the guards for some eggs or a loaf of white bread – luxuries not only to us but to the Italians as well. When we wanted to barter we had to give twenty-four hours notice so that the articles required could be obtained.

One of the rooms on the ground floor in the courtyard had double doors and was known as the Music Room because it contained a piano. It was from there that we decided to get 'Kiwi' away. On the morning chosen for the escape we would wheel our cart into the Music Room and leave it while we collected the rubbish. On returning with the rubbish, 'Kiwi' would be waiting with a sack which he had obtained from the cookhouse. This presented no problem because most of our food was supplied in sacks. We would then place him in the sack, leaving the neck open, and put him in the bottom of the cart and cover him with the rub-

62

bish, making sure that we left a channel for air to get through.

Twenty-four hours before the escape, notice would be given that we wished to do some bartering and we would give a list of articles required. The two men who spoke Italian best were to be selected for this task. When we were satisfied that all was well, we were to push the cart to the gate to be let out. We did not anticipate any trouble there because the cart was never searched, but to divert attention from the cart the two chosen men were to engage the guards in conversation. The other four men would then press on down the drive at a speed faster than usual, pushing the cart tail first. It was anticipated that the guards would offer some comment at the speed with which the cart was being pushed. They were to be told that we had been delayed in collecting the rubbish and were in a hurry to get back to the castle to watch a game of Volley Ball. It was anticipated that the rubbish dump would be the danger spot and it was essential that the guards were not allowed to come that far down the drive. There was to be no delay in tipping the cart, and setting off on the return journey. That was the reason why it was to be pushed tail first: it would be run into the dump and tipped. Then, in order to save time, the men would turn smartly around and pull it away and back to the castle, shafts first. 'Kiwi' would be placed in the cart with his feet towards the tail and having been shot out would land feet first at an anticipated angle of forty-five degrees, which meant that he would immediately fall flat.

There were two roll-calls each day, one at 8 am and the other at 5 pm. If the escape was successful we were to say at the latter roll-call that 'Kiwi' was ill in bed. We knew that the sergeant of the guard would make a check, so we planned the rather optimistic expedient of putting pillows in his bed to resemble the shape of his body hoping that the sergeant would not pull back the bedclothes. If the ruse was successful we intended repeating it at subsequent roll-calls.

I cannot help remarking on the simplicity of this plan.

There were no tunnels to be dug, no holes to be cut through brick walls and no climbing down ropes from windows. All that was required was a sack, some rubbish and six willing helpers.

'Kiwi' planned to head for a point to the north of Piacenza where he hoped to board a goods train that would take him somewhere near the Swiss border, which he then hoped to cross. I asked him if he was going to take any food with him and he replied that he would not be long enough on the journey to need any, but he said that he might take a few bars of chocolate to eat in case of emergency. He was brimful of confidence.

It was left to him to decide when the escape would take place – all we asked was that he gave us twenty-four hours' notice so that we could tell the guards of our wish to barter.

Three days after asking for our help, he told us that he would like to make his attempt on the following day, so we embarked on the first stage of the plan by giving notice of our wish to barter.

At the appointed time on the following morning we were all ready in the Music Room and when we had put him in the cart, completely buried him and were satisfied that he could breathe, we ventured forth. I must confess that my heart pounded a little as we approached the gate. When we saw who our escorts were to be we could have danced with joy because they were the most talkative and argumentive of all the guards and we knew that the job of keeping them in conversation would be easy. They wanted to know why we were late and complained that they had been kept waiting, which drew from us all a lot of mock sympathy and banter. We were all talking together, while the cart was pushed through the gateway unnoticed.

We soon left our escort behind, and we could tell by the sound of their voices growing fainter and fainter that we were widening the gap. No one spoke a word. On arriving at the dump the tailboard was dropped and the contents tipped out. We then turned smartly around to begin our return journey.

The turn around was done so quickly that, afterwards, no one remembered seeing 'Kiwi' as he left the cart.

In concentrating on what I was doing I had momentarily forgotten the existence of the guards and on looking up from my job of securing the tailboard I was pleasantly surprised to see them walking slowly towards us still engaged in bartering. They were too far away from the dump to have seen the sack tipped out and in any case I think they were too engrossed in what they were doing to notice anything else.

We maintained the same pace on the return journey as on the outward journey but on drawing level with the guards they told us to wait a while because they had not finished their business. I could hardly conceal my elation at the success of the plan, and on reaching the Music Room we all heaved a deep sigh of relief and did a little dance of delight.

'Kiwi' was now on his own but we could still help him by doctoring his bed at roll call. Nothing happened during the day to indicate that he had been caught, so as five o'clock approached we placed the pillows in his bed. The duty officer called the roll and on being informed that he was ill in bed sent the duty sergeant to check. We could tell by the nonchalant manner in which he returned that our ruse had succeeded and after reporting to the officer that he was in bed we were dismissed. If he was not caught it meant that he had at least another fifteen hours before his absence was discovered. The pillows were left in the bed all ready for the eight o'clock roll call the next morning.

It was not successful on this occasion, however, because a different duty sergeant pulled back the bedclothes of 'Kiwi's bed. When he discovered his absence he emitted a terrific yell and came charging down the stone steps from the attic. The duty officer then dashed away to report to the Commandant who came charging in to the castle at the head of his guards. We were counted, re-counted and counted again, and then it was finally accepted that someone had escaped.

If a prisoner escaped, it was not the duty of the camp staff to search for him; that was the duty of external forces. It was only their responsibility to discover how it had been achieved and to ensure that further escapes did not take place in the same way. It soon became apparent that they were indeed baffled. We were kept in the courtyard until 4 pm when they reluctantly allowed us to return to our quarters. They had searched the castle over and over again trying to discover the way of escape but without success. Extra guards were drafted to the camp to reinforce security and also to assist in the search. This continued for a week.

The guards could be seen every day in the grounds prodding and digging for possible tunnels. A constant patrol of the interior of the castle was maintained night and day and anyone who normally slept with bedclothes over his head would have them pulled back to confirm that the bed really was occupied. We were not allowed to leave the castle to dispose of rubbish, not because we were suspected of having taken part in the escape, but so as not to hamper the search, and to this day I do not think that the Italians discovered how it took place.

Nothing was heard of 'Kiwi' until the fifth day after his escape when we were told that he had been re-captured and was being brought back, but it was some time before we got the full details. He had been caught while attempting to cross the border into Switzerland and on being brought back to the camp had been put in the cells, but as he was suffering from severe frostbite in both feet he was taken to hospital where he unfortunately had to have his toes amputated. This upset me no end because, having had a hand in the escape, I naturally wanted it to succeed and because I felt it was worthy of success. It was no mean achievement to have reached the Swiss border. I found it extremely sad that he had lost his toes because he was too good a man to be crippled in such a way. However, I still felt that it was the duty of all prisoners of war to escape and those who made an attempt were striving to do their duty.

When it became apparent to the Italians that they were not going to discover how 'Kiwi' had escaped, in order to prevent further escapes, we were all moved to another camp.

IV. ESCAPE

Our new camp was in a small village named Fontenallata, a suburb of Parma. Like the castle, it stood in the foothills of the mountains and commanded a good view of the Plains of Lombardy. Of the Italian officers from the castle, only Prevadini accompanied us to this new camp. The others were sent to the battlefields for having allowed the escape to take place.

The building was four storeys high and contained rooms of varying sizes. It was difficult to say what it had originally been, but it was apparent that it had been hastily prepared as a prisoner-of-war camp. It was encircled by the usual double barbed-wire fence and elevated sentry boxes, and at the rear there was a field to be used for recreational purposes.

Shortly after our arrival Ron and I went for a walk in this field which was used for football games. I happened to kick something hard and on looking down I saw a pair of wire cutters lying in the grass. They had evidently been mislaid by some careless individual engaged in erecting the barbed-wire fence. In a flash I dropped down beside them and, after taking bearings from objects around me to mark their position, I buried them in the ground. They would surely come in useful for future escapes!

An incident occurred at this camp shortly after our arrival that illustrates how trigger-happy our guards were. It was the practice for most of us to congregate on the sunny side of the building on most afternoons to do a spot of sunbathing. On one of these occasions one of our men, who had become mentally ill and was confined to the sick quarters, suddenly emerged from the building, dressed in pyjamas, and before we realized his intentions he approached the barbed-wire fence with the obvious intention of scaling it. One of our company rushed towards him to pull him back. I instinctively looked towards a nearby sentry box to see what the guard was going to do and I observed that he was about to take aim with his rifle. I immediately bent down to pick up a stone and, aiming for his head, I threw it at him. The aim was too low and I hit him on the arm causing him to drop his rifle and, before he could climb down to the ground to retrieve it we had bundled the sick man inside the building. It must have been obvious to him that no one in his right mind would attempt to escape in broad daylight, dressed in pyjamas, and in full view of an armed sentry. The two of us involved in this incident were marched off to the cells and on the following morning appeared before the Commandant. On telling him our story we were dismissed and the guard was punished for his stupidity.

It was now the early part of 1943 and from our daily news bulletin, prepared by an alert American war correspondent who was with us, it seemed evident that the war for Italy was drawing to a close. We heard, in turn, of the shattering of the Axis forces in North Africa, of the Allied invasion of Sicily, of the fall from power of Mussolini and the rise to power of Marshal Badoglio.

There then followed a period of suspense when no news at all was received in the camp and this led to conjecture and supposition amongst us.

On the morning of 8 September we realized that something untoward had happened when we heard the villagers cheering in the street outside the camp and saw some of our guards throw down their arms and walk away. We could get no information about what was happening but in the early afternoon the Senior British Officer was asked to meet the Commandant and on his return ordered us to assemble in the largest of the rooms. He said that confusion and chaos reigned everywhere in Italy and he had not been able to get much information from the Commandant but it was thought that the Italians had signed an armistice with the Allies and that the Allies had landed in Italy. The Commandant did not know what the Germans were going to do, but there were strong rumours that they were going to continue with the war and he proposed holding us in the camp until they arrived to take us to Germany. Ron and I looked at each other with identical thoughts in our minds. We were not going to Germany if we could possibly help it.

On returning to our quarters I looked out of the window and saw that there were no sentries in the sentry boxes. I then went through the building and found that all had deserted their posts except two in front of the building who, instead of manning a sentry box, were now patrolling the perimeter fence.

Remembering the wire cutters, we decided that our way of escape lay through the fence and decided to move when darkness fell. Neither of us knew the exact location of either Genoa or La Spezia, but we assumed them to be on the other side of the mountains, due west of us, and it was our plan to head in that direction, hoping to contact our troops, who, it had been strongly rumoured, had landed there. We anticipated that our journey would take about four or five days and it seemed odd to think that in so short a time we could quite well be on our way home.

Having made preparations, which involved stuffing some concentrated food and personal possessions into our haversacks, we decided in the early evening to retrieve the wire cutters before it got too dark. On looking to see where the guards were, we discovered them to be still at the front of the building deep in conversation with the villagers. We both decided to make our escape at once. We felt that with the coming of darkness the villagers would disperse and the guards then would start their perambulations of the perimeter of the camp, making our escape more difficult.

We went back into the building to collect our haversacks and on our return we observed that they were still in the same place. It was agreed that Ron would keep a watch on the guards while I approached the fence and cut through it. I moved to a position in the centre of the building and after receiving a 'Thumbs Up' I made a dash for the fence and was soon attacking it. I planned to cut a hole two foot square from the ground, and to do so I found it more convenient to lie flat on my stomach. I cut through the inner fence and on receiving a signal from Ron that all was well I crossed the intervening space and was soon assaulting the outer barrier. If I succeeded in cutting through the wire, we had planned that I should make for some bushes surrounding a field some twenty yards away.

Having cut through the outer fence and received a further assurance from Ron that all was well I quickly made my dash and was soon crouching down behind the bushes. I checked the position of the guards and when I was satisfied that we had not been noticed I gave him the signal and he was soon by my side. We then started to climb into the mountains in a westerly direction hoping that it would lead us to Genoa. At last we were in pursuit of freedom.

We had been prisoners of war for a little over three years and as we plodded along it was some time before we realized that we were free. The decision to escape, and the escape itself, had happened with such rapidity that we had moved ahead of our thoughts. So it was in a rather bemused condition that we headed into the mountains.

In escaping through the barbed-wire fence in broad daylight we had achieved what, up to that time, had been considered an impossibility. We could not quite grasp that we had accomplished it and that here we were diving into the mountains at a cracking pace. The roll-call was due shortly after we escaped, but we did not anticipate any trouble because there was no one to whom the Commandant could report our absence.

The area was dotted with little farms and we stopped to speak with some of the farmers working in the fields. When they discovered that we were English, they became very well disposed towards us. Everyone we spoke to was convinced that our troops had made landings at Genoa and La Spezia and we were encouraged to continue with our efforts to contact them.

It occurred to us that if we knocked on the door of one of the farmhouses just before nine o'clock the occupants might allow us to listen to the Nine O'Clock News from London on their radio, even though they had been forbidden to do so on pain of death by the Italian Government. We chose a remote building and knocked on the door just before nine o'clock. Our reception was very friendly and we were soon listening to the familiar chimes of Big Ben followed by the announcement that we were about to listen to the Nine O'Clock News from London. What followed must have gladdened the hearts of millions of people but I must confess that it filled us with dismay. Italy had capitulated and the Allies had made landings, but not at Genoa and La Spezia, as we had been led to believe, but at Reggio di Calabria some 600 miles to the south-east of our position. The occupants of the farmhouse seemed as disheartened as we were. I think that they expected our troops to come charging down the mountainside at any moment.

Ron and I were now in a right old mess. Our plan to contact our troops by crossing the mountains towards Genoa had misfired and, being without an alternative plan, we did not know quite what to do.

The farmer told us of a village named Bardi which lay deeper in the mountains where everyone spoke English and he suggested we go there to seek advice and help. We agreed to go and rose to leave but he pointed out to us the folly of travelling in the mountains by night; he gave us some food and invited us to spend the night in his barn. We gratefully accepted his invitation and soon fell into a deep sleep. We were roused before dawn because the farmer was anxious for us to leave before the possible arrival in the area of the Germans. After thanking him for his hospitality we set off for Bardi.

We had been walking for about three hours when we noticed an old man standing by the roadside ahead of us. On drawing closer to him he suddenly recognized our battledress and began cheering like mad. He was obviously under the impression that we were the advance party of the Allied Armies and in order to silence him we had to confess that we were just two escaped prisoners of war, which damped his spirits somewhat. It then occurred to me that if he had recognized our uniforms others would do so, and it was therefore essential that we obtain other clothing as soon as possible. I asked this old character if he had clothing that he was prepared to exchange with us and he invited us to go with him to his cottage. When we arrived he produced his wardrobe through which we rummaged. Ron was lucky; he found a complete suit to fit him and a shirt, but all that I could find was a pair of Plus Four trousers, an odd jacket and a torn shirt. We donned these clothes but our boots, which were also Army issue, still advertised the fact that we were British and they had to be exchanged as well. For my part this was a foolish thing to do because I received a pair in exchange that were totally unfit for mountain climbing – of which I had a lot to do.

Continuing on our way we discovered that our change of clothing had been worthwhile as we attracted far less attention. We travelled only by day and at night we sought refuge in one of the farmhouses. Although the people were poor and had very little food for themselves they always managed to find a little for us and allowed us to shelter in their barns. They were all anxious for us to be away before dawn the next morning because of the possible arrival of the Germans. If they had been caught sheltering us, the penalty would have been death. Our journey to Bardi was arduous because of our inexperience in mountain climbing and also because of the three years we had spent as prisoners of war which had taken their toll. Every muscle in our bodies ached and we were glad whenever night came so that we could lie down for a few hours to rest.

In deciding to go to Bardi we made what, I think, was our greatest mistake: the journey took us three days and it was during that time, when the confusion caused by the capitulation of Italy and the Allied landings was at its height, that we should have tried to get out of the country rather than waste time in seeking advice. During these three days vulnerable points had been left unguarded by the Italians and had not yet been taken over by the Germans. If we had given the matter more thought we might have opted to head for Switzerland, where I think we would have experienced no difficulty in crossing the Frontier.

Bardi was a small village of twenty cottages or so, where, for some unaccountable reason, all the inhabitants spoke English with a strong Welsh accent! We were made very welcome and were given food, but no one could spare the time to speak to us because we had arrived during the day when everyone had work to do. Shortly after our arrival we were surprised to see one of our fellow prisoners of war from the camp come striding into the village. He was a soldier and if I remember rightly his name was Ogden. Apparently he had seen us escape and had been following closely in our tracks ever since. When the villagers finished their work it was quite late and they were too tired to talk, but they offered us accommodation for the night in a cow shed – which we gratefully accepted.

Early next morning we were amazed to see some more of our fellow prisoners arrive at the village, and a steady stream trickled in throughout the day until there were more prisoners of war than villagers. It seems that on the morning after our escape the Commandant had sent for the Senior Officer and told him that the Germans would be arriving shortly to take over the camp. He had changed his mind and was not now going to hand the prisoners over but was going to desert his post and leave them to their own fate. The Senior Officer had then marched everyone away from the camp in an orderly manner saying that when the Germans arrived it was his intention to march everyone back again to

74

surrender. This, he said, was to avoid possible bloodshed. Many of the men, however, having been marched away from the camp were not prepared to return and when a halt was called to await the return they had carried on marching. They had then taken to the mountains and, like us, had been advised to make for Bardi. The fame of the English-speaking people of Bardi had spread far and wide!

The village was now hopelessly overcrowded and as we could not expect any help or advice, Ron, Ogden and I decided to head south-east in an endeavour to meet up with troops who, we imagined, had already started to advance northwards. The 600 miles between us did not seem so far.

We had not made much progress, however, before we came across another village where some of the inhabitants spoke English. One particular family, comprising husband, wife and three teenaged daughters, told us that they were very busy harvesting their maize but were short of labour. My mates immediately offered help, which was readily accepted. I was eager to keep going because I had escaped in order to get home to my family, whom I had not seen for four years, and also to get back in the war. I contemplated venturing forth alone but on realizing the folly of doing so I decided to join in with the harvesting, hoping that we would continue on our way when it was done. That was not to be, however, because on its completion they showed no desire to do so and, despite my pleadings, refused to move. Ogden was the prevailing influence here and it had been a mistake on my part to allow him to join us. If Ron had been my only companion I am sure that he would have accompanied me.

We had been in this village for about a week when I was delighted to see two more prisoners from the camp walk in. One was an Army Corporal and the other a Second-Lieutenant. I knew the Corporal and knew that he was not getting on very well with his companion and wanted to part company with him. I asked him if he was keen to get home to England and when he replied that he was, I suggested to him that we team up. Nevertheless, parting company with Ron was a very sad occasion because we had been comrades for four years, both in the submarine and as prisoners of war. I reluctantly bade him farewell.

We had not progressed very far, however, when I noticed that my new companion was limping and when I asked him what was wrong he told me that he had received a kick on his leg while playing football which had festered since leaving the camp. I asked to see the wound and it was not a pleasant sight. It was about three inches long and discharging yellow pus. Without treatment it would get steadily worse and eventually force him to give up. It seemed that my efforts to reach England were destined to be dogged by bad luck.

We met many prisoners from the camp in the next few days – most of whom had been to Bardi and had left shortly after my departure. Some of them were just stooging around, but others were making a determined effort to contact our troops to the south. I could have joined up with any of them but I could not leave my companion to fend for himself.

One of the prisoners from the camp that we met was an army captain and he was accompanied by an Italian army officer. This army captain was very pleased indeed to see me because he said that he had been searching the mountains for days trying to contact one of the sailors from the camp. It appeared that this Italian officer was a deserter and, like us, was trying to get out of the country. He had a friend who owned a yacht that was moored in a small harbour to the south of Genoa and he had unsuccessfully been trying to contact him to ask if he could get him out of the country. It was then that he had met the captain who had proposed that they look for one of us sailors to sail the yacht, as they were not able to do so themselves. They asked me if I would consider joining them in seizing the yacht and sailing her. Although it was a very dangerous undertaking, because harbours are hardly left unguarded in wartime, I was prepared to have a go. My companion agreed to come along, and we arranged to meet the next morning because the Italian officer had to get some civilian clothes. That meeting unfortunately did not take place because when we knocked at the door of a farmhouse later in the day to beg for food and shelter, the farmer told us that the Germans were expected to arrive in the area on the next day and advised us to make ourselves scarce. There was no way of warning the two officers so we had to push off as quickly as we could. This was not as fast as we had hoped because the Corporal's leg had got a lot worse and he had to take frequent rests.

On escaping from the camp I had assumed that with the surrender of the Italian Army my only enemies would be the Germans, but I was soon to discover that Fascists were still active and were just as dangerous as the Huns. We met one such man one morning and he invited us to his cottage for some food. We had told him that we were escaped prisoners of war, as indeed we told everyone that we met, because everyone we came into contact with was very friendly and there was no point in concealing our identity. During the meal he left the table but on leaving the room he did not quite shut the door and we heard him telephoning some German troops about us. I am afraid that we beat him up rather severely and, after wrecking his telephone and shotgun, beat a hasty retreat.

This was an isolated incident but thereafter we were on the alert for any more of these characters. Most people that we met were very friendly indeed and anxious to help us. They gave us what information they could if danger threatened. While they were extremely poor they never refused our requests for food and although the penalty for so doing was death, they never refused to give us shelter at night.

Keeping oneself clean was a problem, particularly as my companion's leg was becoming worse day by day. It was therefore no surprise when he told me one morning that he could go on no longer. We were walking along a narrow mountain road at the time and we sat down to decide what to do next. I had already made up my mind that I was not going to leave him and I told him so, but that did not solve our problem. He had to get treatment for his leg and the only way we could get that, I thought, was by surrendering to the Germans. Having agreed with me that that was the only thing to do, we both started to discuss how it could best be achieved.

In the midst of our discussions we saw two nuns walking towards us. They stopped and inquired what was wrong. I first of all revealed our identity and then told them of my companion's plight. One of them asked to see the leg and on seeing it told us that we must go with them to the convent. She then bent down and took hold of one of his arms, indicating that I must do the same. We pulled him to his feet and supporting him on either side we started to walk. On rounding a bend in the road we saw a small village and in it our destination – the convent.

V. THE CONVENT

THE nuns took us to a small room containing two single beds and the Corporal was told to undress and get into one of them. Sister Maria, who had helped us on the road, soon returned with a bowl of water and bathed the wound. She had no ointment with which to treat it but she did have a piece of white rag to use as a bandage.

As my companion was now in good hands, I felt that I could go on alone with a clear conscience. Sister Maria would not hear of it, however, and told me to get into the other bed and invited me to stay until my mate was fit to travel. One of the villagers then arrived to give us a badly-needed hair cut and shave. We had not brought shaving equipment with us, or even a toothbrush, because we had expected to contact our troops shortly after our escape.

Our next visitor was a man who spoke excellent English with a Canadian accent. He told us that he had lived in Canada but on the outbreak of war had returned to Italy. He said that his name was Alberto and on appointing himself our official interpreter invited us to call on him at any time to solve any language difficulties that we might have. He told us that we were in the village of Fontenaluccia and that the convent was maintained by its priest at his own expense, for the benefit of the aged and infirm of the village. There were two sections, male and female, and in the male section there were two old men aged eighty-two and eighty-four respectively, and a hopeless imbecile named Piero aged only twenty. There were four nuns of whom Sister Maria was the eldest at about twenty-five. Sister Josephine at seventeen was the youngest. They wore brown habits which, I believe, was the dress of the novice and Sister Maria had almost reached the stage where she had to take her final vows.

After sleeping on the hard floor of a barn for the past month it was sheer luxury to sink down into a nice soft bed and I was soon fast asleep. I slept until early on the following morning when Sister Maria came into the room with our breakfast. She also brought us a packet of ten cigarettes to share. Where she got them I do not know because they were in such short supply as to be almost unobtainable, but get them she did and on every other morning thereafter she gave us a packet when she brought our breakfast.

As we had more to do with her than anyone else, it is of her that I shall say most. If there are angels on this earth she was certainly one. The way in which she looked after us during our stay at the convent was indeed remarkable. She always had a beautiful smile on her face and always had a kind word for everyone. She administered the convent in a most efficient manner, and I never saw her ruffled, bothered or perplexed. I found it a pleasure to speak to someone so sweet and pure of mind. Of one thing I was sure – in her chosen way of life she had achieved what most of us find so elusive, and that was complete happiness.

We saw very little of the priest during the day because he was a busy man. He did, however, allow us into his house every night to listen to the BBC News and we were thus able to keep in touch with the conduct of the war. Alberto would attend on these occasions to translate the news for the benefit of those present who could not speak English.

On the morning after our arrival at the convent, when Sister Maria had attended to the Corporal's leg, she told me that I was to go with her and one of the other nuns to a nearby village to try to get some ointment to treat the wound. I was amazed at the speed in which they traversed the difficult mountain paths. It was a two-hour journey to our destination and when we arrived Sister Maria, who was very well known, darted away to return triumphantly with a bottle of medicinal alcohol, which was all she could get. The three of us were then invited to go into one of the houses for a meal and were then given some food to take back to the convent. I think that the idea of taking me along was to get me fed, because this was the first of many such visits that we paid to surrounding villages. It was a problem to feed everyone at the convent and it was a great help if some of us could go elsewhere.

It was not long before my companion's leg was on the mend and when he was allowed up we would sit around the fire with the other male inmates of the convent. There was nothing to do except gaze into the fire all day – we had nothing to read. Piero, the imbecile, would sit with his head bowed, grunting like a pig with saliva dripping from his mouth. He had to be watched because he had the habit of suddenly grabbing the hats off the heads of the two old gentlemen, which they wore all the time, and throwing them in the fire.

In the evenings Sister Maria would arrive for prayers. She would kneel at a table and would perform the ceremony of what I believe is called 'Telling the Beads'. Sister Josephine would sometimes join us and we would have a sing-song when prayers were over. We spent some enjoyable evenings, laughing and singing together, which we used to look forward to.

The days were long for me because I was so eager to get home to England, and there was nothing stopping me except my sense of loyalty to my companion.

One way of passing the time was to pick chestnuts in a grove on the outskirts of the village. On one of these chestnut gathering expeditions, an incident occurred that disturbed me very much. A stranger suddenly appeared and, speaking English with an American accent, asked me if there were any escaped British prisoners of war in the area. Foolishly I replied in English, saying that I did not know. Alberto, on hearing the American accent, joined in the conversation and rather monopolized it. In answer to a question from Alberto, the stranger explained that he was an escaped prisoner of war but when asked from what camp, he did not know. He was then asked more questions and he gave such vague answers that I came to the conclusion that he was masquerading. I was convinced of this when he suddenly produced a revolver and asked if I could fire it, inviting me to take him to some nearby woods to show him how. Coming from an escaped prisoner of war, I thought this a very odd request indeed. He may have been a German or Fascist trying to lure me into the woods to shoot me. Murmuring something about having to get back to our chestnuts, we left him.

If this character was a German or a Fascist and he had discovered my identity, it certainly spelt danger for those at the convent. I resolved to leave as soon as I could. Thus, when my companion's leg had healed, I asked him when he thought he would be ready to continue with our journey and much to my surprise he seemed reluctant to do so. I was extremely angry because I had wasted three precious weeks waiting for his leg to heal, during which time I might have possibly been on my way home. I was back at square one again, in the same position as I was with Ron. During that time it had become more difficult to get out of the country because the Germans had restored order and one now had to proceed with extreme caution.

My relations with the Corporal became very strained and it was noticed by Sister Maria when she came for prayers that evening. She asked us what was wrong and, in order not to upset her, we told her that we had been thinking of our wives and children and had become depressed. She did not say anything then but two nights later she came bursting into our room, bubbling over with excitement, and told us that she had thought of a plan to get us home to England. Her plan was to dress us as nuns and in company with a nun friend of hers from another village take us by train to Rome to the Vatican, which was neutral territory. From there we might possibly be flown home.

It was a brilliant plan and I was agog with excitement and

eager to discuss it, but when I looked at my companion and saw the indifferent look on his face, my enthusiasm was dampened. There were snags to such a venture I don't deny. You cannot dress men as nuns without some preparation and expect to get away with it unnoticed. My mate thought of all the snags and mentioned them to Sister Maria. First of all he said that during the journey our beards would grow and would give us away, to which she replied that she had thought of that and had planned that we take shaving equipment with us and we could go to the toilet on the train and shave as often as we wished. Secondly, he mentioned the size of our feet and said that no lady's shoe would fit them. He was told that this had been foreseen and that we would wear extra long habits which would completely cover our feet. Our fingers had become stained with smoking, but Sister Maria told him that we would wear gloves and, in order to conceal the size of our hands, we would keep our hands clapsed, as if in prayer. Snag number four was our voices which he said would surely give us away, but he was told that we were to keep silent and any talking would be done either by her or her friend.

Whilst this conversation was going on I could see that all her enthusiasm for the plan was gradually being squeezed out of her. It was obvious that she had given it much thought and was keen to put it into practice. I asked her if she would take me on my own, but she refused, without giving a reason. Looking rather crestfallen she left us and did not mention it again.

We were sitting around the fire a few days later when there was a knock which was answered by Sister Maria. A man wished to see us. I went to the door, though it was with a feeling of trepidation that I opened it. I was confronted by a man dressed in civilian clothes but wearing a pair of highly polished British army boots. I knew him at once to be British and when he spoke to me in a West Country accent that I knew and loved so well, I could have wrapped my arms around his neck and hugged him. But he had to be treated with suspicion. There was a possibility that he was an enemy soldier masquerading as British. When I told him that I could not speak English he told me that I was not fooling him because he had known of the presence of two Englishmen in the convent for some time. He told me that he was a soldier and, like my companion and I, had escaped from his prisoner-of-war camp when Italy capitulated. Since then he had been staying in a house in a village on the side of the next mountain. He told me that he had been in contact with an Italian priest who was searching the mountains trying to locate escaped British prisoners of war with the intention of forming them into a party to lead through the mountains to contact our troops. A party of twelve was required and this soldier, knowing the whereabouts of other escapees, was visiting them to get things organized.

I could contain myself no longer and I told him who I was. He went on to say that little was known of this priest. The people of his village did not know him and he therefore had to be treated with suspicion. A meeting had been arranged and anyone interested in the venture was invited to turn up. The priest would be present and we would then have an opportunity to decide whether he was genuine or not. I was certainly interested and promised to bring the Corporal along as well.

I felt on top of the world when I went back into the convent to tell my companion and Sister Maria what had happened. I asked the Corporal if he was interested and he replied that he would come with me to meet the priest but that did not necessarily mean that he would embark on the venture. If it was decided to go along with the plan, I was going to ask Jan – the usual naval nickname for West Countrymen – if I could team up with him. I felt that I had played my part in stopping with my mate while waiting for his leg to heal and now he was fit I felt free to leave him.

Sister Maria knew of the village where we were to go but did not know of a priest who would undertake such a venture and she warned us to be careful.

I may add that at this time the Corporal and I had become more amicably disposed towards each other. This was due to the fact that in thinking over Sister Maria's plan to get us to the Vatican we had overlooked the most important snag of all: what would have happened had the Germans seen through our disguise. My mate and I would have been marched back to a prisoner-of-war camp, but Sister Maria and her friend would have faced a firing squad. That could not be allowed to happen.

Allowing ourselves plenty of time, my mate and I set off to attend the meeting and on arriving at the village we were met by Jan who led us to one of the houses. All the others required to form the party had arrived. Except for an Army Captain from my camp who was very pleased to see me, everyone at the meeting was a stranger to me. There was another officer present, a South African Major, and the others were soldiers. I was the only sailor. It was not quite seven o'clock and as the priest had not yet arrived, we had an opportunity to get acquainted.

When he did arrive I must confess that he impressed me. He was not dressed in clerical garb but wore a grey tweed suit with an open-necked shirt. He also wore a stout pair of alpine boots. He was of slim build and not very tall but he had the appearance of being a tough handful.

He opened the proceedings by telling us that it was his intention to lead us through the mountains to contact our troops fightings in the south. He soon satisfied us that he was a genuine ally and as further proof he said that he had just returned from taking a party through the fighting front, producing as evidence that he had really been in contact with our troops a packet of Players cigarettes and a box of Bryant and May matches, which he proceeded to hand round. Although I do not now smoke I can still taste the sweetness of that cigarette.

We now asked him to outline his plan. He said that on the first day we would travel in a body to allow us to get better acquainted. Thereafter we would travel in pairs at fifteen minute intervals. We would move only by day and at night would seek food at one of the many villages *en route*. We would journey fast in order to beat the expected heavy falls of snow which had not yet reached the valleys. Anyone falling sick or meeting with an accident would be left to fend for himself because one man could not be allowed to jeopardize the chances of the others. On starting out each morning we would be given our route for the day and also where we had to rendezvous at night. This information had to be memorized, not written down.

We were happy with the plan and all agreed to embark on the venture. The priest then told us that we would leave at seven o'clock on the following morning and advised us all to get some rest. Jan said that there was accommodation for us in the village but we could not leave without seeing Sister Maria to thank her for all she had done for us. We asked the priest if his route on the next day would take him through our village and, when he said that it would, we asked if we could join him there. He replied that we could and advised us to be ready at nine o'clock.

On the way back my companion expressed some misgivings about the venture and appeared to be contemplating withdrawal. I told him that I had made up my mind to go ahead and as far as I was concerned he could please himself. I was feeling happier now than I had for weeks, for I would soon be in the company of a group of men determined to reach England and I felt that with the priest to lead us our efforts would not be in vain.

Sister Maria was waiting for us on our return and we told her what had transpired. I thanked her for all she had done for us and said that I hoped to see her in the morning to wish her farewell. I could tell by the expression on her face that she did not approve, but she merely said she would get some food ready for us to take. Then she left us.

We were up early on the following morning and went round the village to thank everyone for their hospitality. On arriving back at the convent just before nine o'clock we were in time to greet the nuns as they came out. We noticed that Sister Maria had been crying and when we asked her what was wrong she said that she had not been able to sleep at all during the night thinking of the dangers that would beset us on the journey. Telling us that we would be shot by the Germans, she started to cry again.

As our future comrades approached the village I thanked the nuns individually for what they had done for us and made my valedictions. I left Sister Maria to the last and as I faced her she pressed a rosary into my hand and uttered a short prayer. I still have the rosary and with the passing of the years it has helped me to retain a picture of her in my mind. She was indeed a fine woman and I consider it an honour to have met her.

VI. BETRAYAL

WE joined our comrades and marched till noon when we stopped for a rest and some food. All that could be seen, stretching far into the distance, were the snow-clad peaks of other mountains that we would have to climb. In peacetime people would rejoice in the beauty of the scene, but to us it was heartbreaking.

After a short rest we continued on our journey and on descending the other side of the mountain we crossed the intervening valley to the next one. It was now about three o'clock in the afternoon and this mountain was the highest in that area by far. It became apparent that in order to reach the top before darkness set in we would have to get a move on.

We continued during the afternoon, finding the going hard because of our inexperience and our poor physical condition. It was not long before we were strung out in two parties of six with the priest well to the fore. The gap widened as the afternoon progressed and it became clear to us in the second party that we would not reach the top before dark. The priest showed no signs of slowing to allow us to catch up. He was being true to his word when he told us that we would have to move fast. We carried no water and when we became thirsty some of us stuffed handfuls of snow into our mouths, which was a silly thing to do because it caused ulcers to form on the inside of our cheeks.

As darkness fell it began to get cold and where previously we had been perspiring, now we began to shiver. It became difficult to see the paths in the dark, and our progress became even slower on nearing the top of the mountain, as the snow became thicker. We finally reached the top at midnight, but where we had expected to find the others waiting for us, no one was to be seen. My mate had collapsed with exhaustion and was lying in the snow. No one had a clue where they were and we could easily have died from exposure if one of the party had not noticed the momentary flash of a torch away to our left. We moved in that direction and eventually found the other party established in a cowshed in which they had decided to shelter. The farmer who owned it had given us permission to sleep there on condition that we left before dawn when a party of German soldiers usually called to collect eggs and milk.

We moved the two cows into one stall and occupied the other, filthy as it was, all lying on our sides facing the same direction like sardines in a tin. The floor was of concrete and our hips soon began to ache and when we wished to turn on the other side for relief we had to do so together at a signal from the priest. We did not get much sleep but we certainly kept warm! During that night my companion decided to withdraw from the venture and return to the convent. I told him that I was going forward and we parted with little regret on either side.

We now had to organize ourselves into pairs and I became Jan's partner, which suited me admirably. It was decided that the priest and the South African Major would lead with Jan and me as the second of the six pairs.

Each couple was shown the route for the day on the priest's map and also our night rendezvous. When everyone was satisfied the priest and the Major sallied forth to be followed by the remaining pairs at prescribed intervals. Our greatest danger lay in the valleys where main roads, railways and rivers had to be crossed, areas that were always alive with German troops travelling to and from the front.

On one occasion Jan and I strayed from the route given to us by the priest and ended up walking along the main street of a busy little town. Quite a number of people were about, but it was only Germans who were a real danger. We started to walk away from the town towards a bridge that led over the river. As we approached, we saw it was guarded by a German sentry at either end. We noticed that they were stopping people at random to inspect their documents. We had to cross, however, to regain our route and get to the rendezvous on time. We nonchalantly strolled onwards and stopped to look in a shop window in which we could see the bridge's reflection. It soon became apparent that our German friends were of an amorous nature, stopping all the young ladies who crossed the bridge. If we crossed the bridge behind one of them we might be able to slip past while the guards were occupied.

Before long, we saw a pretty girl swinging towards us. I felt sure that if we followed her we could not only pass the sentries but the whole German Army as well! We sidled along behind her and were soon approaching the first sentry. Speaking in Italian we heard him ask the young lady for her papers and for a date that evening. She obliged with the first request but declined the second and then continued on her way. Our plan worked to perfection because the same thing happened on the other side of the bridge, and we were able to pass both sentries with impunity. However, I think we sweated more in crossing that bridge than we did in climbing any mountain! It was not long before we were back on course again. That was the only occasion that we got lost and we made sure it didn't happen again.

I found Jan an excellent travelling companion. He was as anxious to reach England as I was and we made good progress each day. We were never far behind the priest and the Major and we occasionally caught glimpses of them as they crossed a valley. On approaching our rendezvous each evening we would hang back in order to give the priest time to enter the village to arrange accommodation for us. On these occasions he would seek out the local priest who would invariably ask the villagers to feed and shelter us for the night. Our priest and the Major were always offered accommodation in the home of the local priest while the rest of us slept in the barns and cowsheds of the villagers. The food we were offered was of the poorest, but it was the same as they were eating themselves and for which we were truly grateful. During his stay the priest was able to give further information about the surrounding area, and plan the safest route onwards. He had not told us our ultimate destination and I was reminded of those occasions in the submarine when she would put to sea with none of the crew, except the Captain, knowing where she was bound. They probably both thought that the less they told the men the less they might divulge to the enemy if captured.

I had lost all track of time but we must have been travelling for about fourteen days when we were told to rendezvous at a certain village at midday the following day. When we arrived there we discovered it to be occupied by a party of so-called partisans. They were a mixture of Italian and Yugoslavian soldiers, all heavily armed and in uniform. The leader was a Yugoslav Army Captain. We were told that we would remain in the village for a few days for a rest, and during that time we would have to conform with the routine of the camp and take our turns at sentry-go. I did not like these men and I liked them even less as I got to know them better. I learned that the villagers had been driven from their homes by these pseudo-partisans, and I felt really sorry for these hard-working, honest people.

Just before midnight I reported to the sentry on duty to relieve him. He handed me his equipment which consisted of an overcoat, two bandoliers full of ammunition, two revolvers in holsters, and a semi-automatic rifle. Besides all that the pockets of the overcoat were stuffed with hand grenades! These gangsters were certainly well equipped to repel any attackers!

At about eight o'clock on that first morning I witnessed the departure from the village of six of these men mounted on horses and each leading a pack-horse. I inquired from one of the remaining men where they were going and I was told that they were going to collect food and stores. When I asked from where I was told that they would enter a village and steal whatever they could lay their hands on. Anyone offering resistance would be shot. Once again I was shocked at the conduct of these men and in order to learn more of them I encouraged my informant to tell me of their activities. I discovered that they were all deserters from their respective armies, most of them having fled before the capitulation. They had met up in the mountains and formed themselves into this band. They lived by terrorizing villages and extorting food and possessions from the inhabitants. They had once attacked a convoy of German lorries carrying ammunition but had stolen the firearms, not to fight the Germans but to defend themselves against any possible assault. They were nothing more than a gang of armed robbers and murderers and as I wanted no part in their activities I told the priest of my misgivings. He was as shocked as I was and promised that we would leave the following day.

Darkness had set in before the gang returned and I was there to see them. There was one more man than the number that set out and one pack-horse less. We were told that the horse had missed its footing in the dark and had gone crashing down the mountainside. It had been killed and it was their intention to go back the next day to recover its pack and to cut up the body and bring it back for food. The extra man that they brought back was a young Italian who, while masquerading as a member of the gang, had been committing lone acts of plunder thereby earning them an undeserved name. He was trussed with a rope and put in the shed in the care of the sentry to be dealt with on the next day.

As soon as it became light enough the same six horsemen with three pack-horses set out to recover the pack and edible portions of the dead horse. They did not have far to go because they were back within three hours. The priest, once again showing his versatility, thereupon appointed himself cook and set about preparing the joints for cooking.

We were informed that the young Italian who had been

brought to the camp the previous night was to be Court Martialled, and we were invited to attend. He was found guilty and sentenced to be shot or to join the gang as a bona-fide member. Needless to say he chose to become a member.

Early the next afternoon the priest told us to get ready to depart and after thanking the gang for their hospitality led us out of the village. As we followed him I sensed an air of hostility. I think that they had expected us to join them but as none of us wished to become robbers and murderers of innocent people there were no volunteers. We travelled for the rest of the day in a body and sought refuge for the night in a village that, it transpired, had recently been plundered by the gang. Two villagers had been shot dead and we thought it prudent not to mention that we had recently left them. It felt good to be back with these simple people once again. The air seemed a lot cleaner.

It was not long after embarking on the second stage of our journey that my feet began to trouble me. My boots started to break up, blisters formed, and when these burst my feet began to swell and cause me pain. I experienced difficulty in putting my boots on in the mornings so I began to leave them on all day and night. After a while I began to feel moisture inside them which I assumed was blood. The pain got steadily worse each day, sharp pains developed in my legs and my knees began to swell. Although sleep had never been easy I was now deriving no benefit at all from a nights' rest and was rapidly approaching a state of complete exhaustion. I knew that I could not continue much longer and, reluctant as I was to do so, began to think of surrendering to the Germans. Jan and I were making slow progress and were often hours behind the others in arriving at the rendezvous. I owed a lot to Jan for enabling me to continue for as long as I did. With words of encouragement he would inspire me to greater efforts and on our arrival at our rendezvous he was always ready with a word of congratulation. He was indeed a good companion.

During our journey I lost all count of time and only knew

what day it was when we went to church on Sunday. We must have been walking for about a month when a very significant day dawned for me. In giving us our instructions the priest took us all to the top of a mountain from which we could look across the intervening valley to the next mountain that we had to cross. It was a formidable obstacle with a sheer rock face which we knew to be unclimbable. Leading from the main road, however, was a smaller road which passed along the foot of the mountain and entered a cleft that cut through the mountain. That was our route. It looked easy, but then we learned that a village in which six Germans were stationed was concealed in the cleft. The priest said that was the only way to negotiate this mountain, as a detour would have added a couple of days to our journey. The priest also told us that the German authorities had offered a reward of 25,000 lire to anyone giving information that would lead to the capture of any escaped British prisoner of war and we would have to proceed henceforth with extreme caution.

As we descended towards the valley I realized that I could not go on any longer and inwardly I decided to surrender to the Germans. In order to avoid putting my comrades in peril, I planned on having a go at getting through the village and, if successful, waiting for the others to pass through and then going back to surrender. I did not tell Jan of my plan because I was sure that he would insist on accompanying me and I had no intention of allowing him to do so. I knew that we would argue about it and we had enough to get on with without arguing. So I kept my mouth shut, intending to tell him when we had passed through the village. Having made my decision I felt happier than I had for days and I found that I was rather looking forward to my surrender because it would bring relief from the pains in my feet and legs which had become almost unbearable.

We were about half the way along the road that led to the cleft in the mountain when we were surprised to see a German soldier and a young girl emerge on to the road. They were obviously lovers and would stop every now and again for a kiss.

We were at a loss as to what to do, but could not avoid them in any way so we had to keep going and hope for the best. It occurred to me that even if the German did not challenge us, the girl might well ask me why I was limping, as others had done before. If that happened we would most certainly give ourselves away, so I had to try to walk without a limp.

Our hearts beat fast against our ribs as we drew closer but they did not even spare us a glance. They seemed completely oblivious of their surroundings. What the German saw in the young girl's eyes was obviously more important to him than the two escaped British prisoners who were passing him by! Congratulating ourselves on our luck we continued on our way and were soon entering the cleft in the mountain.

As we penetrated deeper into the cleft the village suddenly came into view. It comprised some thirty houses, behind which rose the sheer rock face of the mountain. It seemed as though a giant U-shaped wedge had been cut out of the mountain, in which the dwellings nestled.

One little cottage stood apart from the others and standing outside was an old woman of about eighty. Many years have passed since that day but I can still remember her vividly. She had snow white hair and her face and neck were wrinkled with age. She stood at the roadside and her hands, clasped in front of her as if in prayer, were stained blue, as if she had been using a dye or had been crushing grapes for wine-making. We had met similar old women on our travels and had found them to be friendly and kind and anxious to help. We therefore saw no harm in passing the time of day with this one. She returned our compliment and then committed what must have been the stupidest act of our lives; we stopped and spoke to her. Despite the warning of the priest a few hours earlier to proceed with extreme caution, we confessed that we were escaped prisoners of war seeking a safe way through the village. We asked her where the

Germans were and she pointed to the largest building in the village which she said was the school. We then asked her if there was any way round the village other than the one we knew. I think we rather expected her to produce a magic carpet and fly us through. She said that there was no other way but, indicating a path which led through the open ground to the left of the road, added that we might avoid detection if we took it. Looking back over the years I cannot understand why we were so stupid as to stop and speak to her when we were in possession of all the information we required anyway.

The moment we left her she started to hobble along the road towards the village, as fast as her tottery old legs could carry her. We knew at once that she was going to betray us. We followed her progress as she sped along the road and saw her disappear into the schoolhouse. Almost immediately six German soldiers emerged, each carrying a rifle, and, spreading out fan-wise, started to run towards us. They called to us to halt and as we did so we turned to face them. On reaching us they immediately searched us to see if we were armed and had we been I am sure that we would have been shot. Using the butt end of their rifles they then beat us up. My forehead was split open and we were both knocked to the ground where the treatment continued. They derived great pleasure from this experience and when we had trouble getting to our feet they helped us with a few kicks in the ribs. We were then told to march to the village and prodded along with the barrels of their rifles.

VII. PRISONERS AGAIN

WE were taken to the schoolhouse where two chairs were placed back to back, and we were made to sit in them, neither looking nor speaking to one another. Apart from the beating, I was glad to have been recaptured, but I felt a little sorry for Jan. Although it had been my intention to surrender, it had not gone according to plan and here we were both in the bag. However we had only ourselves to blame for our misfortune.

The blood from my cut forehead was still flowing down my face and inside my shirt and my body was aching all over from the beating. I did not know how Jan was faring because any attempt on our part to communicate with each other was met with a shout from our captors.

The old lady's treachery had not been very well received by the rest of the villagers and they gathered outside with gifts of food and wine. I noticed that one of the women had a bowl of water and a towel and it was obviously her intention to bathe my forehead. The Germans, however, refused them entry which caused a number of ugly scenes to develop.

As I sat there on that hot, miserable afternoon many thoughts passed through my mind. I thought of my wife and children and I was happy that at least I would soon be able to write to them to let them know that I was safe and well. I thought of my colleagues and wondered how they were faring. It appeared that the priest and the Major had been successful in getting through the village, otherwise they would have been keeping us company. As for the men behind, it was possible that the next pair, on seeing what was happening, had gone back and warned the others. To this day I do not know what became of them. I have since read of a priest being caught and shot by the Germans in the mountains of Italy for assisting escaped British prisoners of war. I have often wondered if this was the man that led us. I hope it was not.

Jan and I were in a considerable predicament. We had to establish our identity and explain why we were dressed in civilian clothes. I had letters and photographs from my wife addressed to me at prisoner-of-war camps, but whether they would be accepted as evidence that I was formerly a prisoner of war was dubious. There was no excuse for the civilian clothes. On being able to establish our identity satisfactorily there was the unpleasant prospect of returning to a prisoner-of-war camp, and as we were now in the hands of the Germans, I was inclined to think that it might be in Germany.

As far as I could gather there were seven Germans. The senior of them was a Corporal and shortly after our arrival I heard him using a telephone. He apparently was reporting our capture to a higher authority with great relish. My impressions of these, the first Germans I had encountered, were very different from my first impressions of the Italian race. Whereas the Italians had seemed that they were about to burst into song at any moment, these Germans revealed themselves as highly trained and disciplined soldiers, ruthless and brutal, and therefore not to be trifled with.

In the midst of my musings I dozed off and fell from my chair. I was aroused by one of the Germans with a few hefty kicks in my ribs. He told me to get up from the floor and as I did so a German officer and four soldiers entered the school. The officer ordered Jan and me to march outside to the car, into which we were pushed and told to take the two inner seats in the rear. A soldier then sat on either side of us and two more sat on tip-up seats facing us. With an armed escort of one officer and four soldiers, they certainly were not taking any risks of our escaping again.

We were driven back along the route we had taken that morning and as we passed the old lady's cottage I wondered what she was doing then. She may have barricaded herself in her house to escape the wrath of the other villagers for having betrayed us. We also passed the spot where we had encountered the German and his sweetheart and as he had been in the school when we were bundled out I also wondered what his thoughts were. He must have been told of the circumstances of our capture and he therefore knew that he had missed us somewhere on the road. He must have been wild with himself for having let slip the glory of being the single-handed captor of two escaped British prisoners of war. It just shows how stupid one can be when in love!

As we drove along Jan and I were forbidden to speak to one another and any attempt even to exchange glances was met with a shouted warning from our escorts. I could not sit comfortably in the car because I was still stiff from the beating and I was wriggling around a lot. My forehead had stopped bleeding and had left me with a severe headache. I had been rather worried because I had tasted blood and had thought that I was bleeding internally, but it turned out to be the blood that had trickled into my mouth as it flowed from the cut in my forehead.

It was not long before I fell asleep again and I was awakened this time by the frequent application of the car brakes as it wended its way through a little town. The car stopped outside an imposing looking building which we subsequently discovered was a hotel that had been commandeered by the Germans as one of their many headquarters.

We were marched in and halted at the foot of the marble staircase in the foyer. The officer in charge then mounted the staircase and returned a short time later accompanied by a young lady interpreter and another officer. We were asked our names and addresses, our official numbers, ranks and service, and when the officer learnt that I was a member of a submarine's crew he murmured U-Boat and spat on the floor. We were then asked where and when we had originally been taken prisoner and what camps we had been in. Our answers to these questions seemed to satisfy him but when we were asked who had been feeding us since our escape and we said that we had been eating berries and the fruits of the wayside I thought that he was going to have a fit. He went purple in the face and the veins in his neck swelled so much that he had to unbutton the neck of his tunic. When he recovered his equilibrium, he asked if we thought he were stupid. I said that I did not mind what he thought as long as he never discovered who had been feeding and sheltering us. I was thankful that nothing had been found in our possession that would have betrayed those good people.

It seemed that our arrival had disturbed the officer for he suddenly brought the interrogation to a close and returned upstairs with the young lady. This rather surprised me because I had expected more rigorous questioning. Of course, there was always the next day to come.

Jan and I were then taken to one of the hotel rooms which contained two single beds, where a sentry mounted guard over us. He rather surprised us by speaking excellent English and told us that he had been studying at one of our Universities but had been compelled to return to Germany on the outbreak of war. He was a very friendly type but had to be treated with suspicion because there was the possibility that he had been instructed to gain our confidence in order to extract information from us. When he told us that we were at a town called Forli, the position of which I was able to check on a map in the room, I was really surprised at the progress we had made. We were told that we were lucky to have been recaptured because quite a number of escaped prisoners of war had been shot while trying to contact our troops and others had strayed into mine fields and been blown to pieces. There was a wash basin in the room and I was invited to have a wash. When I looked in the mirror above the washbasin, I shrank back in horror. I had forgotten that my forehead had been bleeding and my face was covered in blood. Taking care not to open the wound I had a good wash which brightened me up no end. Jan and I had not eaten any food during the day, but that evening we were introduced to the well-known black bread and sausage of Germany. We asked what was going to happen to us and the sentry seemed sure that we would not remain in the hotel for more than a night. He did not say where we would be taken, but there was a horrible implication that we would be marched out and shot.

By force of habit we were both awake at dawn on the following day and as we no longer had to go trudging through the mountains it was heavenly just to lie in bed. The hotel slowly came to life and we heard the jack-booted soldiers walking up and down the corridor outside the room. We also heard them calling to one another in their harsh guttural language which was so different to the soft musical sound of Italian. At about nine o'clock a Corporal and two soldiers came into the room and told us to accompany them. We were marched out of the hotel to a waiting car which moved away immediately. Our journey was of about five minutes duration, then the car stopped abreast a door in a high wall over the top of which we could see the roofs of a number of buildings. We were escorted to the door which was opened by a man dressed in the uniform of an Italian prison warder. No time was lost by the Germans in handing us over. They did not even bother to step inside the door, but turned round and drove off immediately. The door was locked behind us and Jan and I thus became inmates of an Italian civil prison. The warder took us to the reception office where on the desk I saw the biggest book that I have ever come across. It was about three feet square and about six inches thick.

Some difficulty was experienced here in giving our particulars because the clerk could neither speak nor write English. Although Jan and I could make ourselves understood in Italian, we could not quite make out what information about ourselves he required. After studying the questions, we offered to enter our own particulars in it and good progress was made until we came to an item that puzzled us. After giving it careful thought we came to the conclusion that the information required was the maiden name of our grandmothers. Why that information was needed I do not know but on feeling that a little touch of humour would not be amiss I entered Annie Laurie as being the maiden name of my grandmother and Jan, who was blessed with two grandmothers, entered Nell Gwynne and Jane Eyre!

When our task was completed the clerk thanked us for our co-operation and the warder led us away to a cell. A more dismal place than the interior of that cell is hard to envisage. It measured approximately fifteen feet by fifteen and was devoid of furniture. The walls were of white-washed brick and the floor of concrete. The window was set too high to look out of and two bags of straw on the floor were our beds. I do not think that I have ever felt more wretched than I did standing in that cell on that miserable day. The cell itself was enough to cause acute depression and I was still feeling the effects of the beating. My only possessions were the clothes that I wore and they would have disgraced a scarecrow. I was still wearing my plus-four trousers but as I had lost weight my legs had become too thin to support them; they were consequently hanging at 'half-mast'. I did not possess even a toothbrush or comb. It was some relief, however, to find ourselves in an Italian prison because we had expected a more severe interrogation and possible punishment for having been caught wearing civilian clothes.

It seemed as if our travels, at least for the time being, were over so I decided to take off my boots. This was easier said than done because they were stiff with congealed blood and every movement I made caused sharp pains to shoot up my legs. I managed it eventually and was shocked at the state of my feet and amazed that I had managed to go on as long as I did. There were no feet to my stockings, they had worn away completely. My feet were covered in blood and like pieces of raw steak. It was difficult to find any part not affected by either burst blisters or chafe. Jan's feet were in perfect shape but he was, nevertheless, feeling as wretched as I was.

The block that we were in was one of many in the prison. It was oblong in shape and contained four floors of cells, each of which led on to an iron verandah that was fixed to the walls on all floors. The middle of the building was a void except for a wire net that was stretched between the verandahs on the first floor. This, presumably, was to prevent any of the prisoners taking their lives by throwing themselves to the stone floor.

Late in the afternoon of that first day the door opened and four other Englishmen, each carrying their bag of straw, came into the cell. We had asked the warder if we could see any of our countrymen and he had kept his word in asking the Governor if we could be put together. These men were also escaped prisoners of war and were all soldiers. Once again I was the odd man out in that I was the only sailor. We were pleased to see one another and got on very well together.

For the first few days we passed away the time by recounting tales of our service life and many battles were refought as we each told of the circumstances leading up to our capture. When all our stories had been told we organized spelling bees and general knowledge quizzes, and as we had no means of verifying the answers, the Question Master's verdict had to be accepted, however much dispute it engendered.

I had reported the state of my feet to one of the warders and it was arranged that I should visit the sick quarters every evening at five o'clock for treatment. I was now walking about in bare feet and my treatment consisted in having my feet painted with iodine, which caused me to jump around a bit, much to the amusement of the other prisoners who were receiving treatment. Some of these men were dressed in civilian clothes and were on remand, while others were dressed in prison garb and were the regulars. I got to know them all and gathered all the news from them which I was able to pass on to my comrades. Smoking was allowed in the prison, if one could get the cigarettes, and I had an arrangement with these prisoners whereby they would save their cigarette ends for me. I would then take them back to the cell and by using toilet paper as cigarette paper I was able to roll cigarettes for us all.

In the door of the cell, at eye level, there was an aperture about six inches square fitted with a sliding panel on the outside and every day at midday this panel would be slid aside to allow our one meal of the day to be passed through. This consisted of either a bowl of vegetable soup or a bowl of pasta, both of which I knew so well, and a small loaf of bread made from maize flour which gave it a yellow colour. Meagre rations to be sure!

Early every morning we also received a ladle of so-called coffee and this, I believe, was made from crushed acorns. All that could be said in its favour was that it was lukewarm. It was on occasions like this that I missed a good old cup of tea! We were indeed fortunate that we did not have to work, because I am sure that we could not have kept going on those rations.

There was another aperture in the cell, about eighteen inches square at ground level in the wall. The wall of the cell was about a foot thick and on the outside of the aperture on the verandah was a sliding iron door that was kept locked. In the aperture itself there was a bucket and we had to use this, in full view of everyone, when answering the call of nature. It was the duty of one of the civilian prisoners to empty this bucket and he would do so early every morning when, accompanied by a warder, he would wheel a tank along the verandah. When the warder opened the door he would remove the bucket and empty the contents into the tank. When the bucket was replaced the door would be re-locked. Whether the bucket was empty or otherwise there was always an unpleasant smell in the cell.

There were no facilities for washing nor for having a haircut or shave.

Our confinement in this civil prison was a clear violation of the Geneva Convention, for as prisoners of war we should only have been confined in a prisoner-of-war camp. There we should have received the same food as the troops of the detaining power, facilities would have been afforded us to keep ourselves clean and wash our clothes and we would have been allowed to write to our families and to receive mail and parcels from home.

Despite the seriousness of the step, we decided to seek an interview with the Governor to state our complaints. Our request was granted and we were all escorted to his office where he listened patiently to our troubles. When we had finished he said that while sympathizing with us, he was powerless to help because we were not his prisoners. He said that we had been sent to the prison by the Germans, with no orders for our detention and no indication of how long we were likely to remain. Any complaints that we had should be forwarded to the German General commanding the area. Whether he did pass on our grievances or not I could not say because things went on just the same and still we remained in the prison. Perhaps the authorities had more important things to think about than the welfare of six wretched prisoners of war!

There was an exercise period every morning from nine to ten and anyone wishing to take advantage of it would be released from the cells to wait on the verandah for the order to march off to be given. For the first couple of days I was not able to accompany my comrades because of the state of my feet and I therefore had to remain alone in the cell. I was glad when they returned and that I was not permanently alone in the cell. Solitary confinement would indeed have been a wretched existence.

The exercise yard can best be described by likening it in shape to a farm cart wheel lying flat on the ground. The rim of the wheel would represent the encircling wall, the spokes would be the walls dividing the compartments, and the hub would be the watchtower. Two armed warders were posted on top of the watchtower where they commanded a good all-round view of the prisoners. Doors in the encircling wall afforded access to the compartments which each accommodated forty men. It was our practice to split up and each go into a separate compartment, where we were able to collect cigarette ends saved for us by the prisoners. On our return to the cell I would break them up and use the tobacco to make cigarettes for us all. I was the only one who could roll a cigarette – most sailors can – and I think I used more toilet paper for cigarette-making than for the purpose for which it was originally intended!

These exercise periods also gave us an opportunity to gather items of news which, in some mysterious way, always creep into all prisons. We were thus able to follow the progress of the war. There was not much room in these compartments for walking but no one seemed to mind, everyone seemed content just to stand there. I think they were as glad as we were to be out in the fresh air away from the smell of the cell.

The six of us managed to keep our minds occupied with our quizzes and spelling bees but we were all glad when one of the warders told us one afternoon that the Germans would be calling for us on the following morning and that we were to prepare ourselves for a journey. There was little preparation to be accomplished because we were all wearing our sole worldly possessions, but as I was now without boots I had to find something with which to cover my feet. I solved the problem by packing them with straw from my bed and then securing it with strips of sacking. My feet had healed by this time but I felt that I could not venture forth into the unknown without some protection, hence the improvisation.

Early the next morning four German soldiers arrived and escorted us outside the prison to a waiting lorry. We drove through towns and villages until the early evening when we arrived at a prisoner-of-war camp at Mantova in Central Italy. We were to learn that this was a transit camp where escaped prisoners of war were assembled for transportation to Germany. It was not a very happy thought, but it was a great relief to know that we were not going to be shot.

This was not an established prisoner-of-war camp and there was consequently no supplies of Red Cross food parcels or clothing, which was a bitter disappointment to us because we were all in a very sorry state.

My comrades and I were among the first arrivals in this camp, but in the next few days there was a steady flow of arrivals and it soon became full. All these men had escaped from their camps when Italy capitulated and, like me, had failed in their efforts to reach England. All the same there were about 600 men finally assembled in that camp and the trouble that they caused the Germans in re-capturing them was colossal. I did not see anyone wearing a British uniform; they all wore civilian clothes, and I even saw one of them dressed as a priest.

If I could have felt happy at that period, I think I was happy to be in a prisoner-of-war camp once again and removed from the civil prison. One at least had freedom of movement within the camp at all times and the opportunity to meet and speak to one's fellow prisoners and not just at exercise periods, as in a civil prison.

We were fed once a day, as in the prison, but as we were now in German hands we received German food. A ration for one day would be a chunk of black bread and a portion of German sausage or black bread and a dish of *sauerkraut*. It was not long before we all contracted dysentery. Jan and I were only mildly affected but some of the others had it badly and it was in that parlous condition that we set off, on the fourth day after our arrival in the camp, on our journey to Germany.

VIII. GERMANY

WE were marched from the camp to a platform of the local railway station where a string of cattle trucks were standing, into which we were loaded, forty men to a vehicle. Up to this time the six of us from the civil prison had managed to keep together but on being loaded Jan and I found ourselves in a different truck from the others.

The door was in the middle of the truck and facing it was a wooden box fitted with a hinged lid. Jan and I entered the truck together and sat on the floor – on either side of the box. I thought that it might contain our food for the journey which I thought would be an ideal place to be. I could not think of a better place to be than close to food. We had a most comfortable seat because our backs were resting against the side of the truck and our shoulders against the side of the box.

When the truck was loaded with its human freight the door was locked on the outside, but it was opened again shortly afterwards and we were each issued with a loaf of black bread and a portion of German sausage. We were told that this was our ration for the journey, but we were not told how long the journey was to be so we did not know how to apportion it.

I was wrong in thinking that the box contained food because when I raised the lid to satisfy my curiosity, I was surprised to find that it was empty. I could not understand why an empty box should be in the truck, but the mystery was solved when one of the men asked the guard how we would manage to go to the toilet. He was told that this was the function of the box. With everyone in the truck suffering from dysentery, it was soon in use and a queue formed. All the other occupants were strangers to us at the beginning of the journey and I think we got to know them better by the appearance of their bottoms than their faces *en route*! Certainly, no one appeared anxious to change places with us.

The guards travelled in a passenger coach in the middle of the string of trucks but they had to take their turn as sentries in boxes situated on the end of each truck, on the outside above the buffers. They must have had a more uncomfortable journey than us because as we travelled north the weather got colder and colder and we at least were sheltered from the wind. Slow progress was made because we were on a main line and were being continually shunted into sidings to allow priority to faster traffic.

By force of habit I studied the possibility of escape but soon abandoned the idea because it seemed an impossibility. The only way out appeared to be through the wooden floor, and when I brushed the straw aside I saw that the floor boards were secured with countersunk bolts that required tools to budge them. In any case there was no room to work as there were sick men in the truck who could not be disturbed. Although I was without boots I was prepared to attempt an escape should the opportunity arise because our troops fighting in the south seemed so near and Germany seemed so far away. I am sure that many men in that truck would have also seized on any opportunity to accompany me. In escaping from the Italians and being recaptured by the Germans one notable event had taken place. I had ceased to be a *prigionieri di guerra* and I was now a *kriegsgefangener*. Of the two I think I much preferred the former because it sounded so much nicer, but the fact remained that I was still a prisoner of war!

The torments of dysentery continued unabated and with the toilet box in constant use, it soon became full. With the jolting of the truck the contents were frequently spilt over us, and when people began to relieve themselves where they sat, it came to resemble a cow-shed. We were travelling as cattle and we certainly smelt like them. On pulling into the sidings the door of the truck was sometimes opened to allow drinking water to be passed in, but after smelling the stench the guard lost no time in shutting the door again. A hole about six inches square in the side of the truck near the roof served as a ventilator, but as there were slats, angled downwards, fitted across it, it did little to purify the air.

On the third morning of our journey, the train pulled into a siding and remained there for an unusually long time. I was curious to know the cause of the delay and climbed on the toilet box to look out of the aperture. The train was standing in a siding in a fairly large station, the name of which I saw painted on a board: INNSBRUCK. We had passed through the Brenner Pass and were now in Austria.

The train steamed on until the afternoon of the next day when it pulled into a siding and the doors of the trucks were opened. We were told to step out on to the platform. This apparently was our destination. Some of the men were too ill to walk and had to be carried by those strong enough to do so.

We formed up in some sort of order and were marched off. Our route lay through a narrow lane in open barren country and as I was carrying one of the sick men on my back I hoped that we would not have too far to walk. My wish was granted when, on rounding a bend in the lane, we were confronted by the familiar double barbed wire fences and sentry boxes of a prisoner-of-war camp. As we passed through the gates a young girl, dressed in British battledress, ran towards us holding a packet of English cigarettes in her hand with the obvious intention of passing them around. But before she could reach us, one of the guards clubbed her to the ground with his rifle and continued to beat her as she lay there. We were powerless to help her because we were surrounded by armed guards who would not have hesitated to shoot had we made a move. It seemed that the favourite pastime of these Germans was to club their prisoners to the ground and beat them insensible. We were to learn that this young girl was a

Polish prisoner of war, of which there were many in the camp. I even saw young boys of twelve who were prisoners. Poland had put everyone capable of fighting, regardless of their age or sex, into uniform and sent them off to the battlefields.

We were halted outside the administrative offices which we entered, in batches of twenty, to give our particulars. When I walked in, the first person I saw was an Australian soldier friend of mine from my camp in Italy. He was one of four men taking our particulars, so he was not able to spare me much time. He did tell me though, that he had also taken to the mountains when Italy capitulated and had been recaptured by the Germans shortly after. He said that this was exclusively an army camp and, as I was a sailor, I would be sent, in due course, to a naval camp. He had no spare clothing to offer me except for a Polish army officer's tunic that was hanging on the back of his chair and which I accepted with gratitude. I badly needed boots but I had the satisfaction of knowing that I would soon be going to a naval camp where I felt sure I would be able to obtain a pair.

When everyone had given their particulars, a British Sergeant-Major arrived on the scene and introduced himself as camp leader. He promised to issue each of us with a food parcel the following morning. In the meantime we would each receive an issue of twenty-five English cigarettes. The sick were taken to the sick quarters and the remainder of us led to a number of huts in a compound where we were accommodated.

The camp comprised a number of these compounds, each partitioned by barbed wire fences. The whole camp was then enclosed by the usual double barbed wire fence with the inevitable elevated sentry boxes, each manned by two sentries both armed with rifles and with a machine-gun mounted on a tripod.

Jan and I were still together and we were put in the same hut. It was devoid of furniture except for the bunks, which were masterpieces of space saving. They were two tiered and made of wood with six sleeping berths on the top and bottom. There should have been twelve boards, each measuring three feet long by six inches wide, forming the base of each berth, but in all of them there were only three because the others had been chopped up for firewood. I used one board to support my head, one to support my hips and the other to support my feet, and with the proverbial sack of straw to lie on I managed to get some sleep. There were many instances of men in the upper berths falling on men below, and as I had foreseen that eventuality I wisely chose an upper berth. I much preferred falling on someone rather than have them fall on me!

There was no hot water but after I had scrounged some soap from a fellow prisoner, I managed to have a bath in some cold water. I did not have a towel so I dried myself with my shirt which, with my underclothes, I also managed to wash. After drying the articles in front of the stove, I dressed myself again and felt a new man. I discarded my jacket in favour of the Polish army officer's jacket, of which I must confess I was rather proud. But with my plus-fours hanging down my legs at half mast and my feet encased in sacking, plus a month's growth of hair on my head and face, I could not quite be described as a picture of sartorial or tonsorial elegance.

There was a system of bartering in this camp between the guards and prisoners, whereby packets of tea could be exchanged for white bread. However, it was not real tea that the guards received, but used tea leaves that had been dried in front of a fire. The tea was in little two-ounce packets and it was the practice to steam open the packets, extract the contents and refill them with used leaves. The packet would then be carefully re-sealed and exchanged for a loaf of bread, which I thought was an excellent bit of business.

Almost anything could be obtained from the guards of all the camps that I was in, in exchange for items from our food parcels or cigarettes. Sometimes we had an item surplus to our requirements which we were able to barter for a loaf of bread or an egg. As cigarettes were a luxury we were able to exchange some of them for food, which was a necessity.

There were soldiers of other nationalities besides British in this camp, and of these Russians and Poles predominated. I was told, although I cannot vouch for its truth, that when a Russian was taken prisoner he was disowned by his country. He did not receive parcels of food and clothing as we did, and his pay was stopped. If he was married, his wife's allowances ceased. He was not allowed to write or receive letters, and when I say that the Germans hated him more than the English it can be realized that his lot was not a happy one. In the compound adjoining the one that I was in, there was a number of these Russians and on the day after my arrival I witnessed an incident which showed me how hungry they really were.

The compounds were regularly patrolled by a German dog handler and his dog. These animals were mainly Dobermann Pinschers and they were trained to kill. The incident occurred when one of these handlers and his dog entered the Russian compound. The Russians were all in their hut and the handler released the dog and sent it to drive them into the open. Shortly afterwards I observed clouds of smoke gushing from the chimney of the hut and this was followed by the skin of the dog sailing through the door to land at the feet of its master. It appeared that the Russians had killed the dog, skinned it, and judging by the volume of smoke gushing from the chimney, were preparing to cook it.

Unknown to me there had been survivors from HM Submarine *Saracen* that had been sunk in the Mediterranean and a few of them had been on the train that brought us from Italy. I did not know them but I soon made their acquaintance and it was quite a pleasure to be among fellow sailors. It was on the fifth day of my stay in this camp that I was warned to be ready, early on the following morning, to move to a naval camp.

Although I was really looking forward to this move which promised a change of clothes, it was a sad occasion as I was to leave Jan. I had trodden a very difficult path and had shared many misfortunes with him. He had been a good companion and when the time came to say farewell I found it hard, but it was somehow achieved and in company with my fellow submariners I left for a new camp.

We travelled by passenger train in considerably more comfortable conditions than on the previous journey. Our destination lay to the north and as the train proceeded on its way, the weather got colder and colder. We missed the sunshine of Italy sorely. I had re-packed my feet with straw and sacking and they were the warmest part of me. After a day and a half the train arrived at a place called Westertimke, about twenty miles east of Bremen. I cannot recall how we travelled from the train to our new home, but I am inclined to think that we walked and so it was that we became inmates of the prisoner-of-war camp of Marlag and Milag Nord.

On our arrival we were interviewed by a German officer who warned us that any further attempts to escape on our part would have very serious consequences. He hinted that if there was to be a next time, we would not be so lucky as we had been on this occasion. The camp, as its name implies, was in two sections. Marlag was the Royal Navy section and Milag the Merchant Navy section. Each section comprised two compounds, one for the officers and one for the men. Accommodation was in wooden huts, each containing twelves rooms with twelve men to each room.

On being admitted to the camp I was delighted to be greeted by those of my shipmates who had not escaped from the camp in Italy, but had been transferred here by the Germans. They took me first to the camp leader to be allocated a room. Then, holding their noses with finger and thumb in mock disgust at my appearance, they led me away to the washplace where I stripped off all my clothes and had a jolly good scrub. From there I was taken to the clothing store, where I received all the clothes I needed. I then went to the barber's shop for a haircut and shave. To complete my treatment, I was provided with writing material with which to write to my wife and children.

The internal organization of the camp was in the capable hands of a Chief Petty Officer of the Submarine Service, whom I knew well, and he performed this task admirably. Besides the clothing store, there was a library, a food parcel store, a theatre and a shop where one could make small purchases of dry goods. The Red Cross Society had sent musical instruments to the camp and as well as a brass band, we maintained a dance band and small orchestra, which all performed creditably. There was also a theatrical party and they quite often put on plays and musical shows. There was also a soccer pitch and teams had been formed and organized into a league. Cup Final Day was quite an occasion!

Food rations were supplied in their raw state and as the Petty Officer cook of the *Oswald*, who was a personal friend of mine, was in charge of their preparation, it was not long before I was established as a cook. The Commandant of the camp was a Commander of the German Navy and he was quite a friendly type. He made a daily inspection of the camp which always finished in the cookhouse. However, the purpose of his visit seemed to be the bowl of soup that he always received, rather than investigation! In one of the conversations that we had with him, he disclosed that he had been a prisoner of war of the English in the First World War and had been very well treated, which perhaps explained his benevolent attitude towards us. Our guards were also of a friendly disposition. They were all German Marines who had passed the age limit for active service and were therefore more responsible and less trigger-happy than the younger men.

To save petrol, transport in the camp was provided by two horses and I well remember two of the tasks that they performed. One was to pull a carriage in which the Commandant rode while he carried out his duties; the other was to draw a tank, mounted on wheels, that contained the contents of the cess-pit system of sewage. When I saw the horses performing either of these tasks, I immediately thought of the other and it was always a source of amusement to me.

When newly captured prisoners of war were brought to the camp, they were isolated from us until they had been interrogated by a visiting interrogator. One of these was the infamous William Joyce, or Lord Haw-Haw. I knew him by sight and I found it hard to believe that such an insignificant runt of a man could cause so much misery and suffering, as he certainly did with his nightly broadcasts. These were received in the camp and no one could avoid listening to them because there were loudspeakers situated all over the place; there was even one in the lavatory. Joyce received his just deserts after the war, when he was caught and brought to England to stand trial for treason. After being found guilty, he was sentenced to death by hanging.

His broadcasts were not the only ones received in the camp, however. We also possessed a clandestine radio, bought from one of the guards for 2,000 cigarettes, on which we listened to the BBC news. A radio receiver was obviously forbidden property and it was therefore essential that we were careful in its use. It was kept buried in the ground during the day, and was only brought to the surface every evening just before nine o'clock. When the news had been received, it would be hidden again. During that time, men were placed as lookouts so that in the event of any of the guards coming into the camp, the alarm could be raised and passed back to the men operating the set. It could then be re-buried in a matter of seconds. One man operated the set and another took down the news in shorthand which he subsequently transcribed into longhand. This was passed to each hut in turn where it would be read aloud to the inmates. After everyone had heard it, the paper would be destroyed. By order of the Commandant frequent searches of the camp took place, but they were not too rigorous and the camp was not unduly disturbed. On other occasions, however, when searches took place on the orders of a higher authority, a gang of expert searchers would come charging into the camp and tear it to pieces. We called these men ferrets, because of their fondness for digging holes, but they did not succeed in locating the radio receiver and as far as I know it is still there!

No attempts at escape took place at this camp while I was there and I think that this can be explained by our longing for the anticipated invasion of France. Everyone thought that when the invasion did take place, it would not be long before the war came to an end and it was not, therefore, worthwhile making an escape.

As events turned out, quite a time elapsed between D-Day and the end of the war, and when it did come our patience was well nigh exhausted.

The female lead in all plays and musicals put on in camp was performed by a fellow submariner nicknamed 'Whacker'. He played extremely well and as he always wore female costumes on such occasions, it can be imagined that in our womanless camp his appearances were always well received. I remember he once danced solo to Chopin's *Nocturne in E Flat*, dressed in ballet costume – a performance that was requested frequently from then on.

He also had a part to play on Camp Cup Final Day which would open with the brass band parading on the soccer pitch to entertain the spectators to a programme of music on the march. The pair of horses and carriage, having been borrowed from the Commandant, would then be driven on to the pitch by one of the prisoners dressed as a coachman. 'Whacker' would be inside dressed as a woman in a flowery summer dress, a wide brimmed hat and high-heeled shoes. He would then alight from the carriage to be introduced to the teams, and start the match.

I well remember on one occasion when he got out of the carriage in high-heeled shoes, tripped and fell to the ground. He was not hurt but as he fell his dress flew over his head exposing thighs and buttocks clad in a pair of woollen winter-weight army-issue underpants, which aroused a burst of laughter and provoked many wolf whistles. Another incident occurred on one occasion when he was kicking off. He forgot that he was wearing high-heeled shoes and took a hefty kick at the ball. Before his foot made contact, his shoe flew off and struck the referee in the face, which meant he had to receive medical attention even before the game had begun!

It might seem from these anecdotes that life at Marlag had a hint of holiday camp atmosphere about it, but this was not a view shared by the prisoners. A prisoner-of-war camp was a grim, unfriendly place set in bleak and desolate surroundings. The function of the Commandant was to hold captive the enemies of his country taken prisoner in battle, not to make their lives pleasurable. Some Commandants were sympathetic towards the prisoners and others were not. We, at Marlag, were fortunate in that respect.

They did very little, however, in the internal organization of the camp to make life any easier for us. The fact that we led a comparatively happy life was due entirely to our own efforts. Entertainment was made possible by men who possessed acting, sporting, or musical talents volunteering their services to the respective voluntary organizing body to the advantage of all in the camp. Had they wished they could have withheld their services and life then would have been very miserable indeed. However, it was not always easy for these men to offer their services. Take Whacker as an example – the impersonation of a female in a prisoner-of-war camp was a very difficult undertaking and came in for a lot of ribald comment from certain sections of the community. But he persevered and provided us with quite a number of memorable performances.

Posters were exhibited in Marlag camp inviting us to join an organization called the British Freedom Fighters which gave any prisoner of war the opportunity to fight against Communism, supposedly the common enemy of both Germany and England. Any man wishing to take advantage of the offer would be released from captivity and sent at once to the Eastern Front. There were no volunteers from Marlag but I am sorry to say that there were from other camps. They were all rounded up after the war and stood trial in England for treason. They received their just deserts when they were sentenced to prison. The uniform worn by these characters was similar to a British Army service dress, with a Union Jack sewn on the right jacket sleeve. On a number of occasions men were seen wearing this uniform outside the camp, but they may have been German soldiers parading for propaganda purposes.

It was at this camp that I discovered my love for classical music and singing. One of the prisoners had obtained a gramophone and records from one of the guards in exchange for cigarettes. It was his practice to give occasional concerts in the theatre and I spent many pleasant afternoons wandering through Italy with Gigli and the Vienna Woods with Strauss.

On most mornings wave upon wave of American bombers would fly over the camp on their way to deliver an attack. They flew in formations of thirteen and were protected by a screen of fighters buzzing around them. It was impossible to count the number of aircraft as they flew overhead but I learnt from the BBC news that 1,000 bombers and 750 fighters were engaged on each raid. It was truly a magnificent sight. They seemed to use the camp as a landmark because after flying over, they would split up into groups and fly off towards different destinations. After completing their missions they would return over the camp on their homeward journey but not, I am sorry to say, in such perfect formation as before. Some had been shot down, others were damaged and limped along behind the main force. Others would suddenly burst into flames or disintegrate in mid-air. In most cases the crews were able to bale out but there were some who were not so fortunate and I saw them crashing to the ground without parachutes.

Bombing attacks were also delivered at night by aircraft of the RAF. We could not see these aircraft, but we could hear them and could identify them by the tone of their engines.

Frequent attacks were made on Bremen and we could clearly see the glow of the fires caused by the bombs.

It was a very happy day indeed when we learnt of the successful Allied landings in France and of Montgomery's push in our direction. We thought that the war would soon be over and that we would be on our way home before long. However, the Germans were far from beaten and grimly resisted our advancing army. Besides receiving the BBC News every night, we also heard news from our guards and we were thus able to follow the progress of the Allies. Our spirits were raised every day as they drew closer and one day in April, 1945, when we heard gun-fire in the distance, we thought that it would merely be a matter of hours before we were liberated. Excitement ran high in the camp but it quickly turned to dismay when one of the guards rushed into the camp and told us to be ready to march within an hour.

Some of the men decided to remain in the camp to await the arrival of our troops and began looking for suitable hiding places. I considered joining them but after giving the matter much thought I decided against it. I was sure that the roll would be called before we left the camp and when it was discovered that there were absentees a search might be made and anyone found hiding shot. If it had been earlier in the war I would not have hesitated, but having reached this far, when home was so near, I thought it foolish to take risks.

Clothing presented no problem now and when I was dressed and equipped with a spare set of underclothes, I was ready for the most rigorous of marches. The Red Cross food store had been opened and we were told to help ourselves. I filled a haversack with good solid food and although it was heavy it was a load that would get lighter as I consumed the contents.

Orders were then given for us to parade and we moved off shortly afterwards. The officer in charge was a Lieutenant Schultz of the German Navy who told us that he would be in charge of our escort of thirty guards and that his orders were to march us away from our advancing troops for as long as possible. He reminded us that we were all trained sailors and would therefore appreciate that having received his orders he had no alternative but to obey them. He told us that some of the guards would be armed and others would have their dogs. If anyone attempted to escape, he would not be shot but the dogs would be loosed. The two camp horses and the wagon standing nearby would accompany us and be used to carry the sick.

We marched from the camp in an orderly manner but it was not long before we were staggering along in small groups, with big gaps in between. Quite a number of fighter aircraft were flying around and one Hurricane passed so low that we could see the pilot in the cockpit. The officer prisoners had also been ordered to take to the road and left a short while after the men. They soon caught up with us and began to overtake us. As they did so the scream of a fighter aircraft's engine could be heard in a dive. Our two horses took fright, whereupon a Commander of the Royal Navy leapt to their heads to pacify them. As he did so the fighter appeared out of the sun and on levelling off opened fire with its cannon and killed the Commander and the horses.

We were stunned by this attack. Had the fighter been German it might have been understood, but to be attacked by one of our own aircraft was unbelievable. Our surprise quickly turned to anger when we saw the Commander lying dead in the road and we stood cursing the fighter as it disappeared into the distance. We requested permission to bury him but it was refused and when we demanded the right to perform the burial, the German Lieutenant threatened to order the guards to open fire on us if we did not obey. This was indeed a tragic occurrence and it was a profound shock to leave one of our comrades lying dead in the road.

We had not gone much further when we were subjected to another attack. We heard the now familiar scream of the engine as the fighter dived out of the glare of the sun and we stood still waiting for it to appear. We were in open country, with nowhere to dive for shelter, and as the aircraft came into view all we could do was to lie flat on our stomachs in the road. The pilot opened fire on us again and I saw holes caused by cannon shell appear all around me. When the attack was over we rose to our feet with the exception of one man. He had been shot in his head and there was very little of it left. What was particularly sad about his death was that he had been a prisoner of war for over five years and had to die when freedom was so near. Once again we had to march on and leave him lying in the road unburied.

We were attacked on many more occasions but, fortunately, without further loss of life. I shudder to think what would have happened had the pilot attacked us along the road instead of across it. There would have been very heavy loss of life indeed. As we marched along the roads we passed dozens of burnt-out vehicles, mostly German army lorries and cars, and plenty of dead animals. It appeared that the pilots were attacking everything that moved.

Our route lay through agricultural country and seemed to have been planned to avoid cities and towns. We marched in fairly leisurely fashion throughout the day and at night we slept in the open fields or in the outbuildings of a farm. We were indeed fortunate to have brought our own food because we received nothing at all from the Germans. We encountered many road blocks that had been set up to impede the advance of our troops and these comprised deep trenches dug across the roads, giant tree trunks placed across the roads and concrete posts set up everywhere. We suffered very little delay in overcoming these obstacles, but it was different for our troops coming up behind with their tanks and other vehicles.

News was denied us on this march and although we knew that our troops were coming up behind us, we had no idea of their exact location. We knew that we were approaching the River Elbe and hoped that they would catch up with us before we reached it, but that was not to be. We crossed this wide river by ferry a little to the north of Hamburg – the last trip that the ferry made before it was sunk to prevent it from falling into the hands of the advancing Allied Armies.

One advantage of crossing the Elbe was the cessation of the fighter attacks. It seemed that they were attacking targets on the west side of the river only. Our march finally ended at the seaport town or Lübeck where we were marched into a German cavalry barracks, to find our officers already there. We had been on the road for two weeks and what with the airborne attacks and inadequate sleep we had just about had enough.

These barracks did not resemble a prisoner-of-war camp at all. In place of the barbed-wire fences there was a low wall and there were no sentries posted. No felt the urge to escape because we were all awaiting the arrival of our troops. We did not have long to wait because on the third day after our arrival, we once again heard the sound of gunfire.

The barracks lay some distance from the main road and soon stream upon stream of Allied tanks and other vehicles could be seen speeding along the road. I watched them for an hour or so and I began to think that our presence was forgotten until I observed a solitary jeep being driven through the main gate of the barracks. The crew comprised an Army Lieutenant, a Corporal and a private soldier, all from the British Army. They were our liberators.

I had often dreamed of my liberation and when it did occur I must confess that it was something of an anti-climax. I did not quite expect my liberators to be preceded by a brass band, but I had imagined something more spectacular than a jeep! The Lieutenant called for the Senior Officer to step forward and after they had conferred for some time a call was made for the German General to come forward. This rather surprised me because I did not know that there was a German General in the barracks and I was even more surprised when he put in an appearance.

I do not think that I have ever seen a more resplendent figure than this man. It seemed as though he had dressed himself in all his glory for this, his moment of surrender. He wore a greatcoat buttoned to the neck, the collar of which was festooned with gold thread, and when the wind blew it open at the bottom I saw that it was lined with crimson silk. His badge of rank was worn on each shoulder, also in gold. His peaked cap was high in the crown and on the front was the badge of an eagle, looking majestic with its plumage picked out in gold also. As he was a cavalry officer he wore highly polished riding boots and spurs.

The Lieutenant was not impressed by all this splendour, however, because after accepting the General's revolver, he was ordered to sit on the bonnet of the jeep and was driven away ingloriously. Despite the fact that he was a German, I must confess that I felt a trifle sad at the humiliating exit he made from the barracks.

It was surprising how calmly our liberation was received. There was complete silence, as if the situation was beyond our comprehension. Our brains did not seem to function fast enough to understand quite what had happened. The senior British Officer addressed us and informed us that we were no longer prisoners of war and henceforth would be subject to the Naval Discipline Act. We were to remain where we were until transport arrived to take us to an airfield whence we would be flown home to England. He told us that if we wished we could go for a walk in the town, but having made so many unsuccessful attempts at escape I discovered that now I was free to go out of the gates I had no desire to do so.

Later that day a British army lorry arrived bringing food and newspapers, and also a supply of writing materials to enable us to write home. We were told that our letters would be sent by express delivery, but something must have gone wrong, because I accepted my own letter to my wife from the postman at home one week later!

Two days later a fleet of Army lorries arrived to take us to an airfield. A platoon of Royal Engineers travelled in the leading lorry and they made short work of removing and overcoming most of the obstacles *en route*, although some presented more difficulty. I remember the lorries crossing a river via a bridge that had been constructed by lashing planks to the tops of empty fifty-gallon oil drums.

We eventually arrived at an airfield at Luneburg where no one knew anything about us. There was one lone aircraft on the runway and that was a damaged Dakota with one wing. The senior officer of the airfield then made a telephone call during which it transpired that we were to return to an airfield at Lübeck. On our arrival there, we were delighted to find a fleet of Lancaster bombers waiting on the runway. No time was lost in getting us aboard and we were soon airborne.

I had been the first into my aircraft and I was directed to the nose where I found a hole in the deck which was used by the bomb aimer. By lying flat on my stomach I had a good view of the country beneath, and as we flew over Hamburg I was appalled by the devastation that had been wrought by the Allied bombings. I could not see one building standing unscathed. No roads were discernible because they were all buried under thousands of tons of rubble. It was certainly a city of the dead.

When I returned home and saw the damage caused by the German bombings, it was some consolation to me to know that Germany, too, had had its share – and a bigger share than England. As the aircraft continued its flight over Holland, I was once again appalled by the devastation. Vast flooding had occurred where the Germans had breached the dykes and the aircraft flew over miles and miles of water with just the tops of trees and houses showing above the surface.

After flying over the North Sea, I saw the familiar white cliffs of Dover: my first glimpse of England. Shortly afterwards the aircraft landed at Leighton Buzzard. From the aircraft we were conducted to a hanger where I suffered the indignity of being deloused. I had prided myself on being able to keep myself clean and free of lice all the time that I had been a prisoner of war and here I was at the end of the journey being deloused!

From the airfield we were taken in lorries to Waterloo Station in London. It was VE Day plus one, and the streets were packed with thousands of cheering people. On arriving at the station we entrained for Portsmouth, where we arrived at two am. Later that day I went home on leave – after an absence of five years and nine months – to a wife who hardly knew me and to my twin daughters, aged eight and a half who knew me not at all.

RATOON BY CHRISTOPHER NICOLE

When she ordered the flogging of Jackey Reed, the slave who caused her father's death, Joan Dart unwittingly released a torrent of long-repressed emotion, overwhelming the colony in bloodshed and violence. Jackey Reed was a man with a cause – and a burning lust for a white woman's body . . .

RATOON is the explosive novel of men and women deeply attracted to each other and forbidden to express their feelings except in terms of sadism and cruelty. It tells of the powerful passions unleashed by a black rebellion – passions that within forty-eight hours transformed a single colony into a living hell on earth.

0 552 10076 5   65p

DRAGONARD BY RUPERT GILCHRIST

For the first time on the Caribbean island of St Kitts, an English-man has accepted the position of professional whip – master to the African slaves . . . the hated *Dragonard*. But for Richard Abdee it was the beginning of a new life . . . . a life of power, of violence, of lust – a life in which he intended to rule everything and every-one around him . . . both black and white . . . in a society where a thin layer of respectability barely covered the seething currents of sadistic passion and overpowering greed underneath . . .

DRAGONARD is the first in a fast-paced, deeply-moving and, unavoidably, shocking trilogy by Rupert Gilchrist.

0 552 09941 4   95p

A SELECTED LIST OF
WAR BOOKS PUBLISHED
BY CORGI